Around SCOTLAND by BUS

Robert Grieves

Bus conducting is undoubtedly an almost extinct profession as we approach the millennium. Over the last quarter century one person operated buses have all but ousted the last of the dying breed. Passengers, particularly the elderly, felt a greater degree of security with the presence of a conductor, who often also had a smile and time for a few friendly words. Here we see Western S.M.T. conductress Mary Smythe issuing a ticket from her 'Setright' machine on a Kilmarnock local service in the 1950s; a simple scene but one which is fondly remembered.

To Christopher and Alison

Front cover: The Isle of Arran is justifiably known as 'Scotland in miniature' because of the diversity of its scenery. The transport scene was equally diverse for many years, with each fleet having its own distinctive livery; today however, all Arran buses are owned by Stagecoach. Turning the clock back to the summer sunshine of an August afternoon in 1965, an A.E.C. Regal with Lennox of Whiting Bay climbs through the heather hills heading for its home village and leaving Brodick Bay behind, with Goatfell rising in the distance. This bus had started life in 1950 with A1 Service of Ardrossan and carried Scottish Aviation bodywork, built at Prestwick Airport.

Back cover: The back cover features a contemporary advert for Alexander's 'Royal Blue' coach tours as they were known during the 1930s (even after the introduction of the famous 'Bluebird' motif in 1934.) The artist has depicted one of the many Leyland Tiger coaches then in the fleet.

INTRODUCTION

There have been many books published over the years on buses which have dealt with just about every aspect of the subject. Books exclusively on buses in Scotland have been fewer and have tended to deal with the more up-to-date scene. In an attempt to redress this, *Around Scotland by Bus* tries to cover something for everyone from Lerwick to Berwick, albeit looking at the bus scene through mainly nostalgic eyes. Personally I have always believed that the buses of yesteryear had much more character than their counterparts of today. Perhaps my book will convey something of these qualities to younger enthusiasts in particular. I hope so.

Obviously we can only skim the surface of the subject but this is the first in a series which will take a closer look at past operations in all parts of Scotland an area at a time. Hopefully you will enjoy this taster and come back later when the second helpings are available.

Robert Grieves

Contents

First published 1998

ISBN 0 946265 28 3

© Robert Grieves

Typeset and printed by Cordfall Ltd, Glasgow

Published by
Bus Enthusiast Publishing Company
5 Hallcroft Close, Ratho, Newbridge, Midlothian, EH 28 8SD
Bus Enthusiast is an imprint of Arthur Southern Ltd.

The northernmost of the Shetland Islands and accordingly of the British Isles is the Isle of Unst, seen in this view at Uyeasound in the mid 1950s when the local bus operator was J.G. Hunter of Baltasound. AMS 240 was an S.M.T. bodied Bedford OWB originally destined for Alexander of Falkirk but never operated by them as it entered service in 1945 with Leask of Lerwick who sold it to Hunter in 1954.

The longest established bus operator in Shetland is John Leask of Lerwick, the island capital. Caught in the heavy snows of 1955 when the main road from Lerwick to the south mainland became impassable was his only Bedford OB/Duple Vista which had to divert via Scalloway and Gulberwick Junction in order to reach the island airport at Sumburgh. SL 3474 was a 1950 example of the OB type which was replaced later that year with the introduction of the SB model.

Another member of Leask's fleet was SY 9964, an early edition of the Duple Vega bodied Bedford SB, new to Hunter of Loanhead in 1951 and brought to Shetland six years later. It is seen in the late 1950s at Toft pier connecting with converted fishing boat *Shalder* (also owned by Leask) which operated the ferry service north to Ulsta on the island of Yell.

Scalloway on the west coast was the former Shetland capital. This view from the late 1930s looking down on Scalloway Castle shows SB 3866, a 1931 Chevrolet 14 seater owned by James Johnson of Scalloway climbing the twisting hill road above the bay on its service run to Lerwick and about to meet a Chrysler car. Johnson acquired the Chev. in 1938 and sold it to Watt of Reawick in 1945. This was one of the very last models before Bedford replaced the Chevrolet in 1931.

Despite being in a remote part of the British Isles, Orkney was home to a fleet of buses in Edwardian times known as the 'Orkney Motor Express' which connected the 15 miles between Kirkwall the island capital and Stromness via Fintown. Almost incredibly for 1906 this Leyland 'X' type double decker was part of the fleet, long before such vehicles were seen in many important southern cities. Captured on service, S678 appears to be carrying only one upper deck passenger. Bodywork was by Milnes, Voss of Birkenhead, better known for building tramcars; indeed the reversed spiral staircase (which must have obscured the driver's nearside vision) is reminiscent of tramcar practice.

As we have seen, Orkney's first double decker was a Leyland and the last 'decker on the island was also of this make. Between times there was a gap of 60 years with only single deck operation until in 1970 James Peace of Kirkwall purchased EST 392 from Highland Omnibuses along with ECK 934 from Ribble Motor Services. The former was a Strachan bodied Guy Arab which had been new to the Highland Transport Co. in 1951 while the all-Leyland bus was a 1948 example. Both are seen at the end of their brief two year operation on Orkney where they simply rusted away after withdrawal from service.

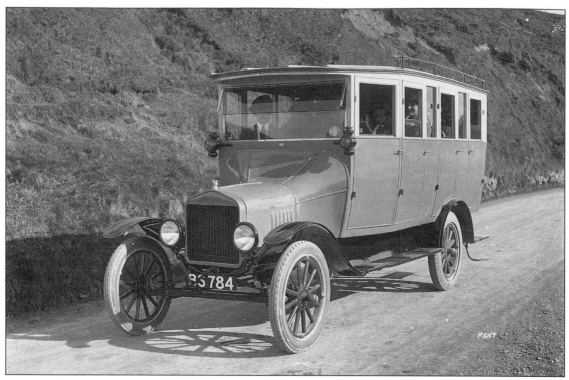

The ubiquitous model T Ford served multi purposes. BS 784 was the third bus in the fleet of Robert Nicolson of Kirkwall, who introduced the first *permanent* service to Stromness and also to Scapa, where it is seen in the mid 1920s. Its 14 seat body was locally built by Harvey of Stromness, who constructed many of the buses and lorries in Orkney over the years.

John G. Nicolson inherited his father Robert's business and continued to operate until selling up on retiral in 1963. The Bedford OB type with Duple Vista bodywork was a popular choice in Orkney and here we see a 1946 example squeezing through the narrow main street in Stromness as it approaches the end of its run from Kirkwall. Today the majority of Orkney services are provided by James Peace, who also operates coach hire in the Aberdeen area.

Highland Independents

Across the stormy Pentland Firth from Orkney to the Scottish mainland lies the county of Caithness. Here at John O' Groat's on the north east tip of Scotland in the mid 1980s we find a Duple bodied Ford of 1980 with Dunnett of Keiss who had provided the service to the old county town of Wick for many years. Today this service is operated by Inverness-based Highland Countrybus.

This busy scene in Wick High Street at the Market Place shows the buses of four of the small owners who served the surrounding country districts in the late 1920s. On the left is SK 1467, a Bean of Walter Wares, Castletown, who operated there via Watten, Bower and Thurso; centre are SK1231, a Chevrolet with Dunnett of Keiss and a partly visible bus with Allan, Gillock. Prominent on the right is Chevrolet SK 1468 bound for Thurso via Kirk, Bower and Castletown, probably owned by Johnston of Castletown.

The now defunct Sutherland Transport and Trading Co. Ltd. had been based in Lairg since 1920, continuing the mail and passenger services pioneered by William Wallace of the Sutherland Arms Hotel which had radiated to far flung outposts of the county. A garage and large retail store in the village were also owned by S.T.& T. thus explaining the company name. Bedford NS 5024 had a specially built 16 seat body by S.M.T. Sales & Service of Edinburgh which incorporated a large compartment for goods and mails and is seen when new at Lairg Station in 1962.

The S.T. & T. garage at Lairg in the late 1950s with miscellaneous members of the red and cream liveried fleet including Leyland Comet artic NS 3939 whose headboard reads 'Buy Loch Clash Fish, Silver Minch Brand'. The buses are DRS 843, a Leyland Comet/Plaxton on the Bettyhill run; NS 1910, a Bedford OWB which served Scourie and Albion NS 2392 for Durness.

Over the years, Highland Omnibuses absorbed several rural operators along with their vehicles and services. One such example acquired in 1965 was the Achnasheen Hotel Company whose main route departed the railway station at Achnasheen to serve a remote area of Wester Ross through to the coastal villages of Gairloch and Laide. Climbing through Glen Docherty with Loch A' Chroisg in the background and bound for Aultbea is Bedford FGS 872 which received Highland fleet number CD 10. The capacity of the Duple body was reduced to 14 seats because of a mail compartment at the rear.

An earlier example of the Achnasheen Hotel Company fleet was JS 3024, a Commer Invader of 1929, pausing at the Kinlochewe Hotel en route for Poolewe and Laide. Just visible behind is a small model A Ford with Spurling body operated by McLean of Torridon between Kinlochewe and Torridon, a service later acquired by McLennan of Diabaig and nowadays run by a Royal Mail post bus.

Among the first bus services in Scotland were those provided in connection with their own rail routes by the Great North of Scotland Railway Co. Ltd. who inaugurated a run between Ballater and Braemar in May 1904. This view of the Main Street in Tomintoul, Banffshire (the highest village in the Highlands at nearly 1200ft) shows SA 875, a Milnes Daimler with open bodywork which was built by G.N.S.R. at their Kittybrewster workshops in 1912. It operated between Tomintoul, Glenlivet and Ballindalloch station. Seems as if the village has turned out to watch while the driver poses for the photographer.

It should not be forgotten that since 1968 the Post Office has been a public transport operator throughout Scotland, mainly serving areas where more conventional services are unable to be provided economically. Usually their vehicles are minibuses but in some instances 4-seat estate cars such as this Chrysler Avenger are used. This scene in 1981 at Culrain, Ross-shire shows the postie with his 'bus' on the Strathoykel mail run.

There is nothing new, however, and long before the Post Office operated their own mail buses, there had been tendered postal services provided by private firms. In 1911 this Albion wagonette owned by Stuart of Pitlochry ran the mail and passenger service between there and Kirkmichael.

A similar mail and passenger service linked the Kirkmichael area to Blairgowrie via Strathardle and Bridge of Cally and this was operated for many years by John Harper of Blairgowrie who also held the mail contract for the Blairgowrie to Glenshee service. GS 9881 was one of two Rolls Royce limousines which were converted to mail buses in the late 1930s by McMurray & Archibald of Perth and seen with driver Willie Slidders at Enochdhu post office. Busy days warranted the addition of the trailer.

Skye Cars (Sutherland of Broadford) operated weekly between Portree and Glasgow using the now defunct ferry from Kyleakin to Kyle of Lochalsh. In the 1970s this service (which had been originated by Neil Beaton of Portree) was acquired and continued by Wallace Arnold. Pride of the fleet in 1966 was OGA 30, an A.E.C. Regal 1V with Burlingham Seagull coachwork making good progress Glasgow bound up the steep and tortuous Carr Brae on the old road from Dornie, closely followed by Bedford SB/Duple WMV 261 duplicating. Eilan Donan Castle is just visible below on the shores of Loch Duich.

Almost insignificant amongst the majestic surroundings, former Wilts. & Dorset Bristol FLF Lodekka JMR 821F makes its way along the single track road en route from Plockton High School to Kyle of Lochalsh, with the mountains of Wester Ross behind. This was owned by Clan Coaches of Kyle in the 1980s who nowadays apart from operating local and schools services both from their mainland base and also on the Isle of Skye, run the 'Skye Ways' express service between Uig on Skye and Glasgow (the forerunner of which is seen in the upper view on this page).

Island Independents

Starting us off on our journey down through Scotland's Western Isles is a wartime Bedford OWB of Mitchell's Bus Service, Stornoway, seen at the harbour in the 1950s about to depart for Ness at the northern tip of Lewis. Parked adjacent to MacBrayne's mailboat is one of the vans used by the Highlands and Islands film guild to bring cinema shows to rural areas.

Also in John Mitchell's two tone blue fleet was AV6600, an Albion Valkyrie bodied by Walker of Aberdeen. This had been new to Sutherland of Peterhead in 1934, passing to Mitchell in 1948 and is seen arriving in the town at South Beach with the island's only cinema, the Playhouse, beyond. Mitchell's services ceased in 1980 and have since been run by several Lewis operators.

The other main operator in Lewis during the post war decades was Hebridean Transport which started as a consortium of several small owners in 1946. Their red and cream buses connected Stornoway with the villages of the Eye Peninsula, locally known as 'Point'. At the town terminus on South Beach in the late 1950s when the fishing industry was still thriving is Bedford/Duple CUX 589, which had previously worked in England with Jervis of Wellington.

En route from Stornoway down to Tarbert on the adjoining Isle of Harris is HCA 177, a Duple bodied Bedford SB with John Morrison of Northton, who had acquired this route from Mitchell of Stornoway. At this point the road climbs away from Loch Seaforth and over Clisham, the highest mountain in Harris. Also in this 1967 scene is a Bedford VAS 1 coach on one of MacBraynes 'Hebridean Holiday' extended tours. 370 FGB (66) was one of their original Duple Bella Vista coaches delivered in 1962.

At Lochboisdale on the Island of South Uist, two Duple bodied Bedfords with MacDonald of Howmore await the evening arrival of the MacBrayne vessel *Claymore* from Oban in August 1962. On the left is OB DTL 772 with SB FVH 411 alongside. Both still carried the liveries of their previous owners as image was seldom a priority in the Hebrides.

The jagged outline of the Cuillin Range makes an impressive backdrop to the village of Ose on the west side of the Isle of Skye. Heading to Glendale from Portree is BST 138, an 18 seat Walker bodied Austin in the smart two shades of green borne by the fleet of Neil Beaton, Portree, who served most parts of the island until relinquishing his bus services in 1952.

In 1946 the Scottish Co-operative Wholesale Society took over the services previously operated by the Skye Transport Co. of Portree and continued to use this name. The Co-op maintained the business for 12 years before selling out to David MacBrayne in 1958. The last bus purchased by S.C.W.S. was this 1952 Albion FT 23 with bodywork by Harvey of Strathaven, seen at Kyleakin Pier. It became no. 50 with MacBrayne and later also ran on the Islands of Islay, South Uist and Mull until withdrawn in 1966.

The small 'capital' on the Isle of Mull is the attractive harbourside community of Tobermory. Climbing steep Back Brae to the upper part of the village is 1935 Commer SB 4688 with Neil MacGillivray, Dervaig who ran between Tobermory and Calgary on the west coast during the 1950s. Stewart of Wishaw built the 12 seat body for Alex. Cowe of Tobermory, the original owner. This was the first conventional bus to operate on Mull.

Alexander Cowe was proprietor of the MacDonald Arms Hotel, Tobermory and also owner of a mainly Bedford fleet which operated island tours and the stage service to Salen and Gruline until acquisition by MacBrayne in 1964. Here we see big Alex. himself with 3 of his Bedfords and an Austin on Main Street in 1949. (SB 7264 had 'I know where I'm going' painted above the windows)

Before the introduction in 1964 of the MacBrayne car ferry linking Oban on the mainland with Craignure on Mull, the Sound of Mull mail vessel had to lie out in Craignure Bay while a small boat ferried passengers to and from the pier. This 1960 scene shows M.V. *Lochnevis* offshore while Bertie Bowman's Bedford ASB 51 awaits custom on his service to Bunessan and Fionnphort for Iona Ferry.

Time to talk before boarding the bus. The Isle of Tiree lies to the west of Mull and is considerably smaller and flatter. In 1960 it boasted only two buses, one of which was FRY 719, this Whitson bodied Commer seen uplifting pupils from Cornaig school. The owner was MacLean of Scarinish.

MacBraynes buses served the Isle of Islay from 1941 until 1972 when the Scottish Bus Group, represented by Highland Omnibuses, continued operations for a short time to be followed by the Post Office, Maroner of Lochwinnoch, Western Scottish and Midland Scottish. This Leyland Leopard had previously worked with Paton of Renfrew who sold to Western in 1977 and YL8 is seen in 1982 at Port Askaig pier awaiting boat passengers for the journey to Bowmore (note the Islay Western Scottish fleetname.)

Today's bus services on the whisky isle are provided by the green and white Mundell's Islay Coaches. A nice touch is the naming of individual buses in this fleet. Mercedes 'The Maid of Port Charlotte' awaits the approaching Cal-Mac ferry *Isle of Arran* from Kennacraig on the mainland Kintyre peninsula before journeying across the island from Port Ellen to Port Askaig.

The Island of Bute has suffered a downturn in fortunes over the years as the once-huge influx of visitors, especially from the Glasgow area, has declined. In 1914 this solid tyred Daimler 40 h.p. charabanc (SJ 142) was bought by McKirdy & McMillan for service between Rothesay and Kilchattan Bay. Note the conductor clinging to the back step – it was his precarious task to balance on the running board and collect fares on the move.

Bute in the late 1950s was still busy with holidaymakers and day trippers. The Rothesay Tramways Company which had operated both trams and buses on the island was acquired in 1949 by Western S.M.T. who then enjoyed a 45 year reign until Stagecoach took over in 1994. On a rainy day in Rothesay we see a line of Western buses at the pierhead in the late '50s, headed by XS 4104, a former Young of Paisley Northern Counties bodied Leyland Titan TD4 of 1936 vintage.

The front cover depicts an A.E.C. on the Isle of Arran: much more typical there, however, as on most of the Scottish islands, was the Bedford. This wartime Duple bodied OWB of 1942 had come from Kia Ora of Morecambe to Stewart's Motors of Corriecravie. In their cream and blue colours it is seen in the early 1950s passing through the village of Kildonan on the southern shores of Arran, to connect with the mainland steamer at Lamlash, despite the destination 'Private'.

MacBraynes for the Highlands

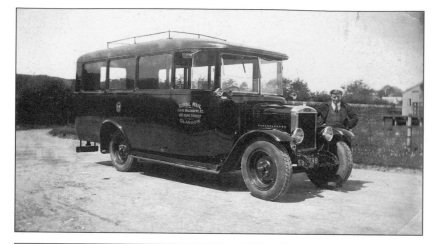

Whenever one thinks of public transport in the Scottish Highlands and Islands, the name MacBrayne immediately springs to mind. Among the wide variety of buses used over their 65 years of operation, Morris Commercials were popular in the 1920s. SB 2698 was delivered in 1926 for the Ardrishaig to Inveraray mail service, with driver Calum Campbell in attendance. At this time the livery was all-over post office red with the 'Royal Route' crest on each side. The lettering reads 'Royal Mail, David MacBrayne Ltd., 119 Hope Street, Glasgow.'

From the 1930s onwards, MacBraynes territory expanded as they acquired a succession of Highlands and Islands operators, usually with only a few buses which depending on condition were not necessarily used. Following the first take-over, Link Lines of Glasgow in 1932, Shields of Kinlochleven was next in 1934. Seen at the garage inherited by MacBraynes in the aluminium smelter village are 20 seat Dennis WM 3843 and 14 seat Beardmore SB 2948. Driver Hugh Cameron (with white cap) remained with MacBraynes for many years and owner John H. Shields became a manager.

Inverness area services to Foyers, Whitebridge and Glenurquhart were operated from MacBraynes depot at Muirtown Wharf on the north bank of the Caledonian Canal, where this early '30s view of assorted Bedfords and Morrises was taken. The leading 3 Bedfords are 49 (ST6957) with Park Royal body, followed by 43 (SB 3833) bodied by Bracebridge of Lincoln with large baggage hopper then 50 (SB 6958). The staff were: Jack MacLean, Alex Chisholm, Sandy and John MacDonald, Eb Ross, Alan Barclay and Angus Ross.

Apart from buses inherited when other operators were bought over, MacBraynes seldom used second hand vehicles. However, in 1936 six of these 14 seat Bedford coaches were purchased from Alexander of Falkirk mainly for touring duties. WG 513 on tour in Glen Nevis was bodied like the others by Alexander Motors of Edinburgh, featuring a folding canvas roof. This one saw further service with the Clyde & Campbeltown Shipping Co. after conversion to a lorry.

Kyleakin pier on the Isle of Skye in 1959, where assorted MacBrayne Thornycrofts and Bedfords for various island destinations await the arrival of passengers from the Inverness train across the water at Kyle of Lochalsh. Leading the line is 79 which was bodied by Harkness of Belfast in 1948 (this bus is now preserved) followed by 147, a 1950 model with contrasting body style by Croft of Glasgow. The Bedfords are two 1952 models with Duple 'Sportsman' bodies and two of the then newly delivered Duple (Midland) examples of 1959.

A question often asked is "How did MacBraynes buses reach the islands before the days of the car ferries?" This photo gives the answer. Here is Croft bodied Commer Commando no. 69 in mid-air being hoisted aboard MacBrayne mailboat *Locheil* at West Loch Tarbert pier in 1948 destined for service on the Island of Islay.

Before MacBraynes Glasgow bus station at Parliamentary Road opened in the late 1950s, all departures from the city left from smaller premises in Broomielaw at Washington Street. The afternoon buses on the Loch Fyne-side service line up here in 1948 led by recently delivered Maudslay Marathon 94 for Campbeltown (140 miles). Duplicating the 99 miles to Tarbert is 68, a 1947 A.E.C. Regal; both carried Park Royal coachwork.

A classic scene from 1951 at Fort William which encapsulates typical MacBrayne operations. This was the year when the company celebrated its centenary but was also one of the few when no new buses were added to the fleet. The mailboat T.S.S. *King George V* has sailed up Loch Linnhe from Oban and approaches the pier where three Maudslays await connecting passengers. 98 and 96 on the right have Park Royal bodies while to the left is Croft bodied 128.

Among the most attractive buses purchased by MacBrayne were three Roe bodied A.E.C. Regals delivered in 1953, which were the last half-cabs in the fleet. On the shore of Loch Linnhe at the 1930s art deco Fort William bus station is no. 27 awaiting departure for Kinlochleven. This bus lost its traditional appearance in 1961 when fitted with a new Duple coach body. It was finally withdrawn in 1970.

Until the upgraded 'Rest and be Thankful' hill road was opened after the 1939-45 war, MacBrayne buses had to negotiate the top hairpin of the old road by making a couple of cuts around this severe bend. This panorama shows two 1938 Park Royal bodied A.E.C. Regals led by no.8 climbing towards the summit in 1946, with a splendid view looking down Glen Croe. The new road may be seen taking a straight course above the old. (See also p. 127)

Former MacBrayne buses were popular purchases with independent operators since they were generally in good condition and well maintained. MacTavish of Arrochar bought two of the 1949 Maudslay Marathons and this view from the bridge of the Loch Lomond paddle steamer *Maid of the Loch* in 1965 as she approaches Tarbet shows GUS 408 for the onward tour connection across the isthmus to Arrochar pier to join the cruise vessel on Loch Long.

Apart from David MacBrayne the other Scottish bus company which has achieved an almost cult status is Walter Alexander, who from humble beginnings prior to the 1914-18 war, eventually became Scotland's largest bus operator, while their Bluebird coaches were synonymous with luxury travel. Typifying the early fleet is MS 2860, an RAF type Leyland charabanc which had been new to Dunn of Denny in 1920 before passing to Alexander.

A 1925 advertisement to publicise Alexanders' Motor Service as the company was then known. It featured no. 45 (MS 6049) a Northern Counties bodied Albion which was the latest member of the fleet at that time. This was the first of four similar 24 seat Albions delivered that year and was the start of a close association with this make for the next decade. Note the mis-spelling of Cumbernauld, shown as Cumberland!

A housewife scrubs her steps in King Street, Stenhousemuir, as a new Thornycroft A1 model passes Haddow's grocers shop bound for Lime Road in Falkirk. MS 7782 was number 11 in the fleet of Hugh Pender, Bainsford who ran both local services and tours, selling out to Alexander in 1931 although continuing to operate as a subsidiary until 1936.

MS 7460 was an impressive Leyland Lioness which arrived in 1927 and had Alexander's own bodywork built at their premises in Brown Street, Camelon. Numbered 78 originally, it later became M1 and is seen in Cunningham Street, Glasgow prior to loading for Aberdeen. The traditionally styled W. Alexander & Sons Ltd. fleet name had then been recently introduced and was to remain familiar right through to the 1960s.

Another Lioness was 194 which later became P88. This was a 1929 model with bodywork by Burlingham of Blackpool incorporating a roll-back canvas roof. The buses and services of Rankin Bros. Glasgow were acquired in 1929 and MS 9111 is seen in the Pass of Brander on the Glasgow to Oban service which Rankins had pioneered. This involved a journey time of 5 hours 20 minutes at that date, compared with a mere 3 hours today.

Leyland Lion PLSC3 MS 7465 was originally 83 when new in 1927 but when this view at Dunfermline bus station was taken in the mid 1930s, it had been renumbered L61. Alongside is a Leyland Lion in the associated General Motor Carrying Co. fleet of Kirkcaldy.

Alexanders had a small depot in West Port, Forfar, the former county town of Angus. A diminutive baby Austin 7 saloon passes by as D4 prepares to depart along West High Street on the Dundee service. This was a 1929 Albion PM28 with body by Dickson of Dundee.

R5 (MS 9189) was one of Alexander's first double deckers. It was one of the popular Leyland Titan TD1 models which took the country by storm in the late 1920s. Delivered in 1929 with Leyland's own bodywork, it is seen towards the end of a long working life in 1948 on a Leven town service at Letham Glen.

A Brechin bound Leyland Tiger makes its way through Laurencekirk, Kincardineshire. This was P4 which had been delivered as 762 in 1931 with Alexander bodywork. The 'P' class of Leyland Tigers eventually achieved a total of 860, the highest number of any Alexander series.

As Alexander built up an empire to become Scotland's largest operator (and in Britain second in size only to Midland Red) the company took over numerous smaller firms. Typical of these was Gibb of Huntly in 1931 who had a fleet of imported American Reos on services in the Strathbogie area of north west Aberdeenshire. This glimpse into Gibb's garage shows SA 9613, SA 9864 and AV 1027, all Reos which joined the Alexander fleet for a brief period.

Barnton Street Stirling in 1933 with MS 8541, a 20 seat Bean new in 1928 to James MacKenzie's 'Wee Bus Service,' pausing to pick up passengers on his local route between Cambusbarron and Riverside. About to overtake is Leyland Tiger P12 of Alexander's, based at their depot in Forth Street, inherited with the Scottish General business. MacKenzie eventually sold to Alexander in 1943.

Former Scottish General (Northern) Omnibus Co. of Elgin Leyland Tiger P66 (SO 3580) of 1929 and Albion C8 (MS 7851) of 1928 stand in Crieff High Street adjacent to Alexander's office in the mid 1930s. There was also a depot in Church Street which had originally belonged to Crerar of Crieff and then Scottish General of Larbert. Both buses carried Alexander bodywork, that on the Tiger having replaced the original in 1934.

The original 'Bluebird' coach was P77 (MS 8670), a Leyland Tiger TS1 which had been new to Scottish General of Larbert in 1929 and transferred on acquisition the following year to Alexander. Its Cowieson body was replaced in 1934 by this new Alexander coachwork painted in the well-known two shades of blue with cream relief and signwritten for the Glasgow to St. Andrew's service. Note the initial style of Bluebird emblem which differed slightly from that adopted later.

In comparison to the original 1930s 'Bluebird' above, this view shows two from the 1980s under ownership of Midland Scottish Omnibuses. MM 647 was one of four 25 seat MCW Metroriders delivered in 1987, while MRM 118 was an Alexander bodied Metrobus with 80 coach seats, also new in 1987

Two Bedfords were acquired from Valentine's Motors of Perth in 1935. GS 3838 had a locally built body by Cadogan of Perth and became W28 with Alexander. It is seen on the summer only service between Perth, Blairgowrie and Braemar, at Alexander's depot in that village, which was originally built for the Great North of Scotland Railway Co. as their bus depot in 1904. The building is still in use today with Stagecoach and thus must surely be a contender for Britain's oldest bus depot.

Alexander's developed long distance services although in some cases had not pioneered them. Seen in 1934 near Slochd Summit, which at around 1400ft is the highest point on the route between Glasgow and Inverness is newly delivered P157 (WG 2361) an Alexander bodied Leyland Lion. The route number blind shows 'limited stop' and it is interesting to compare that the journey time then was timetabled at 8 hours 11 minutes while today's equivalent is 3 hours 35 minutes!

The municipal fleet of Perth Corporation was taken over in 1934 but for some years afterwards Alexander painted the local buses in red livery with the Perth City Transport name. The first to be so treated were three Albion Victors which had been ordered by Perth before acquisition. These had Alexander bodywork and were numbered A5-7, but ran for only 2 years until disposal. A6 is seen when new at Perth City Hall.

Pitlochry depot was home to P565, an Alexander bodied Leyland Tiger TS8 new in 1939. Visible behind the Bedford/Burlingham Seagull is RMG 209, an Albion recovery vehicle purchased from the war department in 1947. 'Py' designated this small depot which served a very rural area and the garage code may be seen below the fleet number plate.

Alexander bodied Bristol LH no. MLH16 operated from Pitlochry depot in the 1970s. It is seen on a local service at the Square in Moulin, an attractive village just outside Pitlochry on the road to Kirkmichael.

Turning from Dundee's Lindsay Street bus station into Ward Road in 1955 is Letham bound P816 (CSF 224), one of several Alexander bodied Leyland Tiger TS8s transferred along with the S.M.T. Dundee area services in 1949. A Corporation tramcar heads to Lochee past a typical Dundee jute mill in the background.

Harris & Sons of Leven sold to Alexander in 1939 with their twelve predominantly Thornycroft buses. Seen in 1935 in wintry conditions near Lathones on the service from St. Andrew's to Largo, Leven and Buckhaven is FG 7276, an A12 type bodied in Fife by Jackson of Dunfermline and which became T38 with Alexander.

The emblem of crossed flags surmounted by a crown was Alexander's commemoration to the Queen's Coronation in 1953. It also pinpoints when the photo was taken in Dundas Street, Glasgow adjacent to the bus station. W81 (WG 8470) prepares to leave on a Trossachs tour and its smart appearance belies the fact that this was a 1939 Duple bodied Bedford WTB. The presentation of Alexander's fleet, particularly the 'Bluebird' coaches, was always of a high standard.

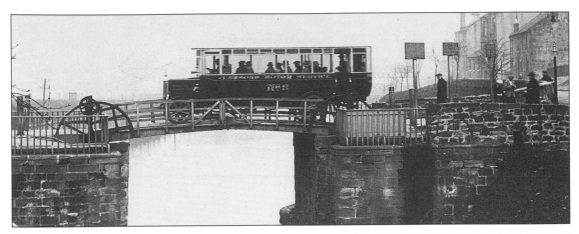

David Lawson of Kirkintilloch built up a number of services linking that area to Glasgow during the 1920s. This atmospheric scene on the old bascule bridge across the Forth and Clyde Canal in the Cowgate, Kirkintilloch shows Lawson's no.8, one of several R.A.F. type Leylands in their fleet. Alexander acquired the company in 1936 but Lawson's retained their identity and a degree of autonomy until 1961 when Alexander (Midland) took full control.

Kirkintilloch Cross in the early 1960s is the location for P658, one of a large fleet of Leyland Tiger TS8 'specials' delivered in 1940 with Alexander 39 seat bodies. This one was transferred to the Lawson fleet in 1949 and is seen on service from Lenzie to Glasgow via Whitegates. Alexander (Midland) had taken over in 1961 and so this bus had been repainted from Lawson red to its former shade of blue.

The 'PA' class of Leyland Tiger PS1 reached 216 between the first deliveries in 1947 and the last in 1950. Most carried Alexander's standard 35 seat front entrance bodywork built at their Stirling coachworks (although the final batch had full fronted coach bodies by Burlingham of Blackpool). PA131 and 127 of 1949 are seen at Oban railway station (now demolished) in the mid 1960s.

The Campsie Fells rise behind the main street in Lennoxtown where a Leyland Titan TD1 in the brown and cream livery of A & R Graham of Kirkintilloch uplifts schoolchildren on its journey from Campsie Glen to Glasgow. SN 4655 (16) had been re-bodied by Cowieson and became R 225 with Alexander when the Grahams sold out in 1938.

One of Grahams' earlier vehicles was SN 2988 a 1924 Reo charabanc seen here bound for Campsie Glen at the Glasgow stance in Cathedral Street on Queen Street Station bridge. It was obviously a fine day as the canvas hood has been folded back to reveal the cloche hats of the period. The schoolboy conductor in short trousers was Jack Graham.

The annual Highland Gathering at Braemar always provided plenty work for Alexanders. This was the scene on the evening of Saturday 4th September, 1952 as all the buses streamed away after the event, those for the south climbing through Glen Clunie towards the Cairnwell Pass and thence over the old Devil's Elbow road and on to Blairgowrie. This convoy is led by A40 (AWG 627) a 1947 Alexander bodied A.E.C. Regal followed by P542 (WG 8121) a Leyland Tiger TS8 of 1939 also with Alexander body. The photographer was my friend the late George Oliver, whose Rolls Royce is prominent in the foreground.

CAV 899 was delivered in 1945 to James Sutherland of Peterhead whose company was taken over by Alexander in 1950. This Duple bodied Daimler was numbered RO 688 and was transferred in 1962 from the Northern area of the company to Stepps depot and on this occasion was operating on a Saturday short working of the Gartcosh route from Glasgow's Dundas St. bus station to Gartloch Hospital. The famous 'Bluebird' logo painted on the wall was still visible until 1997 when new development covered the area.

A different Daimler indeed to that in the previous illustration both in appearance and performance was the 'Fleetline'. Alexander (Midland) did not purchase any until 1967 but between then and 1980 a total of 170 joined the fleet. Alexander bodied MRF164 was a 1980 example and is seen on an afternoon duty in Callander en route from McLaren High School to Deanston.

In 1961 Whyte's Bankfoot Motor Service was acquired by Alexander (Midland) but none of their five elderly Bedfords was retained. Towards the end of operations CES 447 a 1948 OB model with S.C.W.S. bodywork stands in Kinnoull Street at Foundry Lane, Perth. The brown liveried fleet linked the 'Fair City' with Waterloo via Luncarty and Bankfoot 10 times daily.

Pitlochry Motor Company Ltd. was formed as a subsidiary of Alexander in 1929. A.E.C. Reliance GS 1327 with Hall Lewis body was new in that year to Alex. McKercher of Aberfeldy but passed with the Aberfeldy-Pitlochry service to P.M.C. in 1931. January 1932 found it in difficulty on the Perth-Dunkeld-Pitlochry service when the River Tummell burst its banks and the driver may be seen carrying a passenger to dry land.

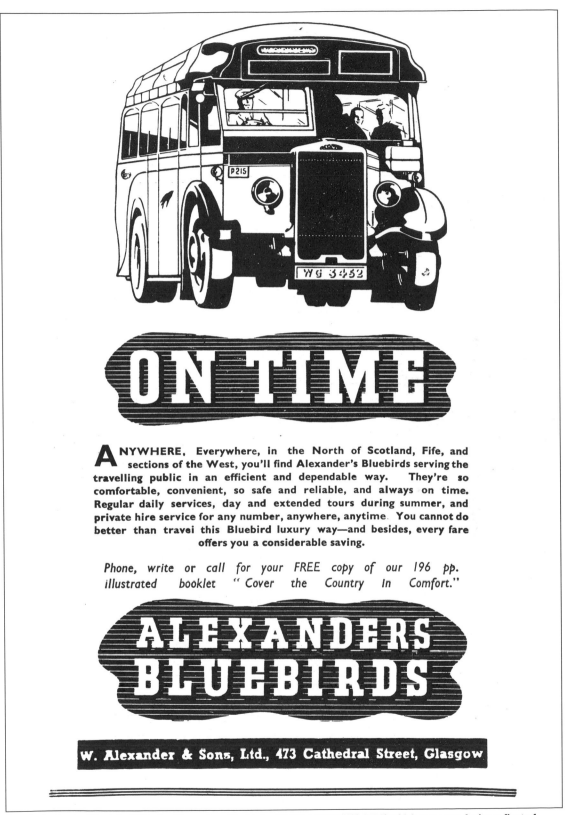

A typical advert of the late 1930s for Alexanders Bluebirds showing P 219 (WG 3452) which was one of a large fleet of Alexander bodied Leyland Tiger TS 7s delivered in 1935.

The initials S.M.T. are still well known today on buses in the Edinburgh area but the origins of Scottish Motor Traction go back to 1905 when the company was formed to operate bus services from our capital city. S 545, one of the original fleet of Maudslay double deckers passes through Livingstone (spelt with an 'E' in those days) in 1907 when the 'Sunday Bus' from Edinburgh was introduced through the village on a service to West Calder.

Maudslay open charabanc S1378 at Waverley Bridge, Edinburgh which is still a bus stance today. The destination board along the roof reads 'Edinburgh/Gorgie/East & West Calder and just below it a return fare of 1/9d (9p) is advertised! This photograph dates from 1912 when S.M.T. suffered its first strike over dismissed drivers who were members of a then recently formed trade union.

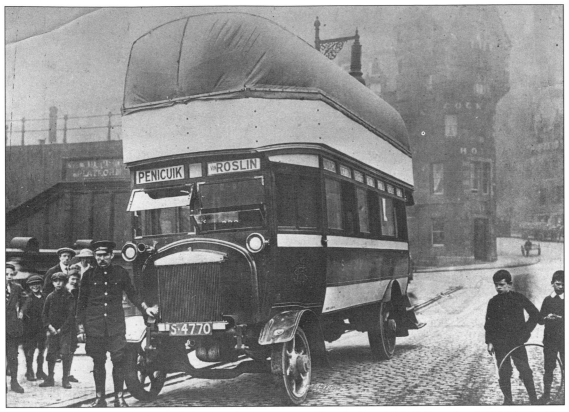

Towards the end of World War 1, petrol shortages became acute and in order to maintain their services S.M.T. introduced coal gas operation, the gas being carried in the balloon on the roof which was refilled at terminal points. S 4770 was a 1914 Lothian (fully built by S.M.T. in their own workshops) thus fitted, at Waverley Bridge stance with the usual assembly of interested schoolboys, those on the right with hoop and stick, presumably not sufficiently affluent for a gird and cleek.

Throughout the 1920s & 30s in their ongoing programme of expansion, S.M.T. acquired the services of many smaller rival operators along with their vehicles (often only used for a short time). Take overs in 1926 included Tennant of Armadale and Hendry of Coatbridge, which enabled S.M.T. to inaugurate a through service between Edinburgh and Glasgow. The oldest bus inherited with Hendry's fleet was solid tyred Leyland VA 1720 of 1923, seen at their Clarkston terminus from where they ran to Glasgow via Airdrie.

As services expanded, so new depots were built, such as this one in the Steelyard at Bathgate in 1923. A 14 seat Beardmore (SF 3797) enters while on the left is one of a large batch of Albions delivered in 1927 with full fronted bodies by Croall of Edinburgh. It has paused on the Edinburgh to Glasgow service for a crew change at the depot, which due to lack of capacity was replaced by one in Whitburn Road in 1931 and now also closed.

One of nine S.M.T. acquisitions in 1931 was John Beuken of Fauldhouse whose main service connected Shotts, Fauldhouse and Bathgate. Eight assorted buses were taken over including three Beans similar to this. SX 2863 waits at Beuken's East End garage when new in 1929 while the driver replenishes the petrol tank.

Expansion in the Dundee area started in 1920. This scene at Alyth shows Albions on the Dundee to Blairgowrie service in 1929. Cowieson bodied RS 8305 on the left was originally with Major Sibley (the Gordon Line) of Aberdeen while SC 570 was a Croall bodied example new to S.M.T. In 1949 these Dundee area services were transferred to Alexander control.

A further purchase in Dundee in 1938 was W.&P. Robertson & Co. who concentrated mainly on private hire and tour work. Most of their vehicles acquired by S.M.T. were Commers, including YJ 3666/7 which became W6/7 seen prior to delivery in 1936 at Cadogan's coachworks in Perth.

The S.M.T. depot in New Street Edinburgh, which opened in 1928, was centrally located just off the Royal Mile. This 1945 scene shows an assortment of various vintages which includes A.E.C. Regals and Regents, Leyland Titans and a newly delivered utility Guy Arab in grey wartime livery, contrasting with the blue of its neighbours.

In 1958 when triumphant cup-winners Hearts paraded their success through the city streets of Edinburgh, the trophy was displayed from the open top deck of J57 (CSF 258) an all-Leyland TD5 new in 1939 and converted in the mid 1950s. This was the first S.M.T. open decker since Edwardian times!

The first new double deckers delivered after the war (and the last in the blue livery which was similar to Alexander's) were 40 A.E.C. Regents in 1948 with rather angular Alexander semi-utility bodies. BB 32 is seen with a stablemate at the Bangour stance in Edinburgh's St. Andrew Square which was a street departure point for most services until 1957 when the present bus station opened nearby.

In 1949, much more attractive Duple bodied A.E.C.Regents arrived, like newly delivered BB69 gleaming in St. Andrew Square sunshine about to depart for North Berwick. These were the first 8' wide double deckers in the fleet and also the first to carry the re-adopted green livery. (S.M.T. colours changed from green to blue in 1930 and back to green in 1949.)

Single deck deliveries in 1949 were A.E.C. Regals with Burlingham and Alexander bodies. An example of the latter is B392 on a multi-bus charter at George Heriot's School in Edinburgh, with the rear of a Burlingham bodied example to the right. B392, along with several others of its batch, received a new full fronted Burlingham coach body in 1954.

St. Andrew Square in 1950 with a variety of buses visible at their various stances, including a 'United' Bristol on service 12 to Berwick and Newcastle. Leaving for Loanhead and Penicuik is LHY 949, the prototype E.C.W. bodied Bristol Lodekka (complete with impressive exposed radiator) on trial in Bristol Tramways livery. Highly satisfied with the results, S.M.T. went on to purchase a total of 256 production models.

Edinburgh folk will remember the chimney of Portobello power station which was a local landmark until demolished in the 1970s. In 1955, a recently delivered A.E.C./Park Royal Monocoach (B483) picks up passengers in Portobello High Street, en route for Seton Sands. Corporation trams had been withdrawn from Portobello services the previous year but in this view the tracks are still in place although the overhead wires have gone.

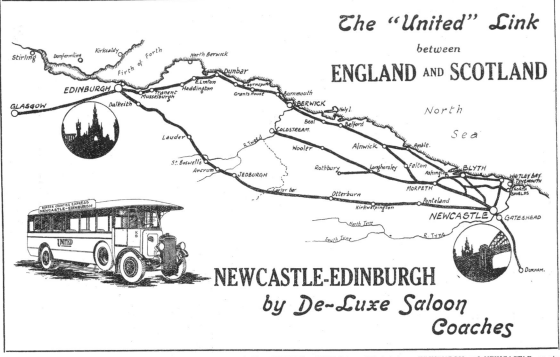

CIRCULAR TOUR: Passengers holding "UNITED" or S.M.T. Return Tickets between EDINBURGH and NEWCASTLE, or vice versa, are permitted to return by "UNITED" or S.M.T. vehicles, also by way of BERWICK or JEDBURGH. A most enjoyable circular trip can thus be made at the Extraordinary Low Fare of— **16/6** RETURN

A publicity map of 1929 showing the joint operations of S.M.T. and United Automobile Services between Edinburgh and Newcastle. The bus depicted is K9 (VF 2834) an Associated Daimler with United's own bodywork featuring a roof route board showing 'Border Counties Express, Newcastle-Edinburgh'. United's livery at that period was yellow.

S.M.T. and United shared town services in the border town of Berwick on Tweed in Northumberland. H 93 (FS 5615) was a Metro-Cammell bodied Leyland Tiger TS6 of 1933 in Berwick bus station which also housed the joint S.M.T. and United garage premises, seen behind. This situation continued until 1994 when successor Lowland Omnibuses relinquished their Berwick services and depot leaving Northumbria Motor Services in full control.

Western S.M.T. Co. Ltd

Now part of the Stagecoach empire, Western was born in 1932 as the S.M.T. company's subsidiary for operations in south-west Scotland. Its major constituent was the Scottish General Transport Co. (a subsidiary of British Electric Traction) based latterly in Kilmarnock. Tilling Stevens had always been a popular choice with this operator and we see four 32 seaters on their delivery run in 1931 from the Brush coachworks in Loughborough. These examples were later transferred to the Rothesay Tramways Co., to serve on the Isle of Bute.

The other major company at the formation of Western S.M.T. was John Sword's 'Midland' Bus Service of Airdrie (Sword became Western's manager). Apart from a network of routes mainly in Renfrewshire and Ayrshire, the Midland flagship service was that from Glasgow to London, then a marathon 16 hour journey. Burlingham bodied Leyland Tiger TS2 coaches pause for refreshment at Allnutt's Templar Cafe in Baldock on their journey north in 1930.

Among the many operators swallowed by Western in the 1930s was Currie & Thomson of Calderbank from whom in 1932 the lengthy service linking Airdrie, Hamilton, Strathaven, Darvel, Kilmarnock and Ayr was inherited (running time 2 hours 45 mins.) VD 529 was a Gilford 1680T seen in Priestland near Darvel bound for Ayr. Today this route is no longer covered by a through service.

CS 3489 was the last member of a fleet of 40 Alexander bodied Leyland Cheetahs delivered to Western in 1936. It is seen en route from Gourock to Glasgow at Renfrew Cross with the town hall in the background. Half of this batch had been built for service with Alexander of Falkirk but diverted to Western.

Ayr High Street with Leyland Titan AG 8233 heading for Lochside. This bus had been the first of a fleet of TD2s purchased by S.M.T. in 1932 to replace the Ayr Corporation tramcars. Initially painted in S.M.T. blue, they were all in the immaculately presented black and white Western livery by the time of this view in 1938.

The last tram in Greenock was no. 10 which made the final run on 15th July, 1929, from Cathcart Square through Gourock and on to Ashton with Provost Drummond at the controls and tramways manager R.B. Herbert alongside. Replacements were open staircase Leyland Titans for Greenock Motor Services built by Christopher Dodson (as in this view), Hall Lewis and Leyland.

In 1949 the local services operated around Port Glasgow, Greenock and Gourock by Greenock Motor Services were incorporated into the Western fleet. At Gourock pierhead shortly before the take-over is Strachan-bodied Leyland PD1 VS 4868 followed by Weymann utility bodied Guy Arab VS 4349, both working with G.M.S. while on the other side of the street at the Glasgow stance is a Western A.E.C. Regent/Northern Counties and a Brush bodied A.E.C. Regal. The poorly constructed Strachan body on the Leyland was soon to be rebodied by E.C.W.

Operations of Tilling-owned Caledonian Omnibus Co. of Dumfries passed to Western control in 1949. Naturally Bristols featured strongly among the vehicles taken over, but other makes such as this elderly Leyland TD1 were also inherited. Numbered 891 with Western it had started life in 1930 with Chatham & District Motor Services, passing to Wilts. & Dorset and then to Caley. It is seen at Western's Carlisle bus station in Lonsdale Street where a variety of display boards outside the office advertise day tours which attracted particularly good business in the 1950s. It closed in 1981.

Caledonian 164/5 (SM9978/9) became 808/9 with Western. They were Eastern Counties bodied A.E.C. Regals new in 1933 and photographed in Abington, the half way stop on Caley's Dumfries-Thornhill-Biggar-Edinburgh route. This service had been taken over along with the business of Harper's Motor Service, Peebles the previous year.

The next important acquisition was Young's Bus Service of Paisley, Scotland's largest independent bus operator, in 1951. A mainly Albion fleet had been built up since the mid 1920s serving Glasgow, Paisley and Johnstone, with links to Largs and West Kilbride. Inside their lofty main garage and workshops in Mary Street, Johnstone, we see part of the Y.B.S. fleet in 1934. The Northern Counties bodied Albion Venturer (no.73) was their first new 'decker and appeared in the Olympia motor show in 1933.

Young's 108 was a 1938 Albion Venturer with Preston-built English Electric bodywork, seen approaching the riverside stance in Clyde Street, Glasgow used by most buses for Renfrewshire and Ayrshire from the city. When the yellow Y.B.S. fleet was repainted Western red, 2000 was added to the former number, this one becoming 2108.

Young's associated operator was the Paisley & District Omnibus Co. which served local routes around Scotland's largest town from a now closed depot in Gordon Street. Guy Arab 295 of 1949 with the attractive style of body built by Guy Motors themselves was one of the last buses purchased by P&D before acquisition by Western. It heads past the Anchor Bar in a largely unchanged Gauze Street, Paisley on the Ferguslie Park-Gallowhill-Arkleston-Lochfield circular service.

Two former Young's coaches seen under Western ownership in the early 1950s on tour in Oban. 2198 was a Maudslay built by Brockhouse of Clydebank in 1949 followed by 2161, a 1947 Bedford OB with coachwork by S.M.T. of Edinburgh to Duple design. All but one of the 13 ex-YBS Maudslays lasted until 1960 with Western whereas the 3 Bedfords were withdrawn in 1954.

Serving Paisley in the mid 1950s, Western 192, a Massey utility bodied Guy Arab of 1943 moves away from the Cross towards High Street alongside Glasgow Corporation experimental lightweight tramcar no.6, based at Elderslie depot. (The last tram ran in Paisley in 1957 although it was a further 5 years before the G.C.T. system finally closed.)

Ardrossan bound 1381 ploughs through floodwater at Linwood Toll, Elderslie between Paisley and Johnstone. This was an Alexander bodied Leyland PD2/20 of 1957 based at Western's depot in Ardrossan on the north Ayrshire coast. 57 Leyland Titans entered the fleet that year.

Also delivered in 1957 were 19 Bristol LS6Gs with Alexander dual purpose coachwork. Greenock based 1276 is seen when new en route from Gourock to Glasgow climbing Hatton Brae on the south bank of the Clyde between Langbank and Bishopton. Dumbarton Rock may be seen across the river in Central S.M.T. territory.

Between 1963 and 1975 Western purchased no less than 316 Leyland Leopards with the familiar Alexander Y type 49 or 53 seat bodywork. 2405 was a 1973 example but following an accident was shortened and rebuilt as a 41 seater for employment on the now abandoned Erskine local service.

Seddons were also popular in the Western fleet. Thornliebank-based 2939 was a 1979 delivery with Alexander T type coachwork working the former MacBrayne service from Glasgow to Tarbert, and thence to Kennacraig where it is seen crossing the causeway to connect with the ferry to Islay.

As did its fellow Scottish Bus Group companies, Western S.M.T. operated some very rural services, often with double deckers, for example between Ayr and Tairlaw Bridge, several miles beyond Straiton. On a dreich December morning in 1965 Alexander bodied Leyland PD3 AD1530 sets off over the bridge returning to the county town. The totally uneconomic section of this route between Straiton and Tairlaw was withdrawn in the late 1960s and many other rural services were later curtailed following the 'Scotmap' exercise of the early 1980s .

EMERGENCY SERVICES

As from SATURDAY, 16th SEPTEMBER, 1939, emergency services will be in operation on all routes. Time Tables on application to Conductor.

THE PAISLEY & DISTRICT OMNIBUS CO., LTD.
YOUNGS' BUS SERVICE LTD.,

'Phone 3191   4 Gordon Street, Paisley

Ex bus-driver Bill Tomkins

You little thought that the driver of your bus, speeding along the leafy lanes or winding a dexterous way through interminable traffic, was qualifying for a key post in war! Yet, that is what Driver Bill Tomkins did, and today he is driving a truck. If his absence and that of many others like him, is causing you occasional inconvenience, do not forget that he is still serving you. He has left his old job to others and although greater demands than ever have been made upon the bus services, they have risen to the occasion with the help of substitute staff in the essential business of carrying the nation's workers.

BRITISH BUSES

ISSUED BY THE BRITISH OMNIBUS COMPANIES PUBLIC RELATIONS COMMITTEE

Bus posters are a fascinating study in themselves. The upper two are examples from wartime. Little did the public realise that the emergency services were to be with them for many years to come.

Help to shape a better bus service **BY FILLING IN A FORM**

Philippa Form SAYS...

SCOTTISH

BUS PASSENGER SURVEY

Philippa Form fronted the Scottish Bus Group passenger survey (Scotmap) of the early 1980s and this poster was often seen throughout Scotland on the windows of S.B.G. vehicles. Undoubtedly many improvements were made as a result of this exercise but at the same time rural services in particular accordingly suffered cutbacks.

Central S.M.T. Co. Ltd

The Lanarkshire Traction Company (formerly Tramways Company) based at Traction House, Motherwell, was one of the main constituents when Central S.M.T. was formed in 1932. Although model T Fords were generally more popular with small independent operators, L.T.C. bought four in 1922, one of which is seen with the 'black squad'. These 14 seaters generally worked the Hamilton to Strathaven service.

A.E.C.s were predominant in the early Lanarkshire fleet. This was one of several solid tyred 'Y' types purchased from the Scottish Transport Co., then based in Coatbridge, which were re-registered (this one VA 7602) fitted with pneumatic tyres and rebodied by Pickering of Wishaw, at whose premises this scene was taken in 1928.

Glasgow General Omnibus & Motor Services Ltd., more usually known simply as G.O.C. was the other major operator in the newly formed Central S.M.T. Co. in 1932. George Square, Glasgow is the setting for no.66 (VA 6483), the first of 93 Associated Daimlers purchased in 1927-8. There were already 65 A.E.C.s in the fleet, all of which and the majority of the A.D.C.s were built by Metcalfe of Romford.

In 1929, G.O.C. took delivery of 20 of the popular Leyland Titan TD1s with Leyland's own open-staircase style of bodywork, although this was later rebuilt to enclosed form. L10 is seen in 1936 in Central's dark red livery in Glasgow Clyde Street at the stance for Busby and East Kilbride (which at that time was only a rural village).

J.W.&R. Torrance was a Hamilton-based company running to Glasgow via Cambuslang and absorbed into the G.O.C. in 1932 shortly before the formation of Central S.M.T. Torrance had built their depot at Burnbank Road, Hamilton which continued to be used by Central for many years. Albion PK26 No.38 (VA 8198) had an Alexander body and became Central's A91. It was on display at Albion Motors stand at the 1928 Scottish Motor Show in Glasgow's Kelvin Hall.

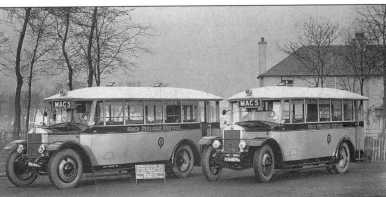

Among the smaller fleets acquired by Central was David MacPhail of Newarthill, trading as Mac's Pullman Service (and still operating coaches today). Rear entrance Albions VA 8247-8 (which became Central A114-5) are seen in 1928 prior to delivery from John Stewart's Coltness Coachworks in Wishaw. MacPhail's two services had operated from Newarthill to Motherwell and to Glasgow

The first buses to be delivered to the newly formed Central S.M.T. were 50 Leyland Tiger TS4s in 1932 which were bodied locally by Pickering of Wishaw. T29 (VD 1701) heads along Cadzow Street Hamilton, bound for Coalburn on route 52 from Glasgow.

The scene is Main Street, Bothwell in 1937 outside Tunnock's tearoom where one of the salesmen is loading his little red van with Tunnock's temptations. The trio of passing buses (even then they came in threes!) is led by Central Leyland Lion F21 (VD 3417) of 1934 on route 51 to Larkhall, followed by an 'H' class Leyland Tiger of S.M.T. on their Glasgow to Edinburgh via Hamilton service (which took 2hrs. 40mins.) and at the rear is one of Central's 'T' class Leyland Tigers of 1932.

T124 was one of 17 Alexander bodied Leyland Tiger TS8s which arrived in 1938. After withdrawal from the Central fleet in 1953 it served for a further couple of years with Western S.M.T. Parked alongside at the Traction House depot in Motherwell is A.E.C. service lorry VA 6669 dating from 1927.

During the war, a few of the so-called 'unfrozen' double deckers were allocated to Central (these were buses built during the restrictions of wartime but with some refinements of peace-time vehicles). All were Leylands except E1, a Bristol K5G which came in 1942 bodied by Northern Counties. This was Central's only Bristol until the arrival of their first 'Lodekka' in 1955.

Leaving the terminus at Newarthill (Biggar Road) on a short working to New Stevenston is H37, a Strachan utility bodied Guy Arab of 1945. In the stance is L478, an all-Leyland PD2 of 1954, destined for Motherwell on route 93. Many of the wartime Guys had a relatively long life with Central, surviving in regular service until 1960.

Central and its associated 'Lanarkshire' fleet (absorbed in 1949) had a large intake of Leyland Titan PD1s then PD2s between 1946 and 1954. Further 'tin fronted' examples arrived until 1960. In Clyde Street, Glasgow, are all-Leyland PD2s of 1948; L354 carries the 'Lanarkshire' fleetname while L420 is 'Central', with both fleets sharing the same dark red livery.

Bristol/E.C.W. Lodekkas were a familiar sight in Central livery and a total of 376 were operated, including some from National Bus Companies in various parts of England which had been exchanged for VRT models which had little success with the Scottish Bus Group. These three views show :

B20, one of the original 1955 batch which featured the long radiator used on early models and seen in Hope Street Glasgow on lengthy service 242 for Peebles which with a journey time of 2hrs 45 mins. was Central's longest route.

B79 which arrived in 1958 heads down Wishaw High Street on busy route 56 from Shotts to Glasgow which at that time boasted a 15 minute frequency from 5 a.m., serving mining and industrial areas over its full length.

The Bonkle bus, leaving Waterloo Street bus station in Glasgow. BL 281 typifies the later front entrance Lodekkas (L signified long) and was one of the 1965 intake. The bus station had been built by G.O.C. in the late 1920s but closed when the new Anderston bus station (now also closed) opened in 1971. And for the uninitiated, Bonkle lies just beyond Newmains, towards Shotts.

A former Baillie Bros. Cowieson bodied A.E.C. Regent of 1933 which Central loaned to London Transport during wartime transport shortages in the capital during 1940 and '41. The camera has captured M2 in Trafalgar Square with the columns of St. Martin-In-the-Fields to the right. It returned home to work with Central until 1948 before seeing further service with Clark of Dumfries then Gibson of Moffat.

Main Street, Alexandria, 1935, with a Cowieson bodied Albion Valiant of Baillie Bros. Balloch-bound on the busy service from Glasgow, especially so with day trippers in fine weather such as this when the sliding section of the roof had been pulled back. Baillies' fleet, latterly based at Hartfield Garage Dumbarton was acquired in 1936 and operations transferred to Central's Gavinburn depot at Old Kilpatrick (closed in 1997). This bus became W41 in the Central fleet.

One of 34 similar Guy Arabs delivered between 1948 and 1952 with Guy's own attractive bodywork incorporating the rear entrance always specified by Central. K29 was one of the last examples and is seen in Quarry Street Hamilton on a local service to Whitehill.

Highland Omnibuses Ltd

The youngest member of the nationalised Scottish Bus Group was Highland Omnibuses Ltd., formed in 1952. It was mainly a combination of the Highland Transport Co. and MacRae & Dick, both based at Inverness. Highland Transport had favoured both single and double deck Guy Arabs for its fleet, exemplified by no. 24 (BST 68) with Gardner 5LW engine and wartime utility Weymann body featuring wooden slatted seats. It is seen at Beauly en route from Dingwall to Inverness in the maroon livery of Highland Transport.

In Strathpeffer about to depart for Dingwall in the late '50s is BST 92, another wartime Guy Arab delivered in 1945 to Highland Transport but seen after acquisition by Highland Omnibuses. E29 differed by having the more powerful Gardner 6 cyl unit and body by Roe of Leeds. Note the British Railways notice board despite the fact that the village had lost its rail passenger service in 1946 with total closure of the line in 1951. The original maroon colours of Highland Omnibuses were very similar to the previous Highland Transport livery.

On Scotland's far north coast in the county of Caithness lies Thurso, our northernmost mainland town. ST 5751 was a 1929 Albion originally in the scarlet livery of Inverness & District Motor Services Ltd. which formed the basis of the newly constituted Highland Transport Co. in 1930. No. 41 at Thurso town hall prepares to depart for Wick via Stemster.

One of the original Ford buses operated in 1925 by Inverness & District where Wilmot H. Fowke, formerly of Chapman's garage in the town, was both general manager and engineer. 'Morning Star' was built by Eaton Coachworks of Cringleford, Norwich with a 20 seat body on an extended model T chassis. It is seen at Beauly on the company's original service between Inverness and Dingwall.

Inverness & District livery was a colourful two shades of scarlet, with cream above. Their no. 30 (ST 4324) was an Albion PM 28 of 1927 which later served with Highland Transport until withdrawal in 1947.

Some of the Highland Transport fleet in Bank Street Inverness when new in 1932. The leaders were 9 &10 (ST 6982-3), both Albion Valkyries with bodywork by Cowieson of Glasgow. No. 9 had a long life, lasting (albeit rebuilt) until the formation of Highland Omnibuses in 1952 when it became A9.

Highland Transport 55 was an impressive Park Royal bodied AEC Royal delivered in 1933. It is seen at Brochie's Corner on the main road between Inverness and Beauly en route for Thurso, a journey which took a marathon 9 hours 30 minutes, but today operates in 6 hours less time since the bridging of the Firths.

No. 76 was a particularly interesting member of the fleet. ST 9465 was a Gilford/HSG (high speed gas) with an A.E.C. 6 cyl. petrol engine and bodied in-house by Highland Transport in their Inverness workshops, entering service in January 1938. HSG was a company formed at the works of the liquidated Gilford Motor Co. in London to develop and produce gas plants for road vehicles. The producer gas unit burned anthracite and not peat as rumoured although this had apparently been considered. This bus was the first in Britain to run on producer gas and proved successful during several years of operation in the Highlands. It is seen here on Drumochter Summit driving south for trials with Glasgow Corporation in 1938. Note also that it carried the Golden Eagle motif which Highland had introduced in the mid 1930s and which has been re-adopted by the current Highland operator.

Apart from the Highland Transport Company the other major constituent on formation of Highland Omnibuses was MacRae & Dick of Inverness. ST 8667-8 were Albion 'Victors' new in 1936 with 26 seat coachwork by Porteous of Linlithgow, which became Ap 101/2 with Highland. Both were regular performers on the Inverness to Fort William service which was shared with David MacBrayne.

MacRae & Dick owned ST 221 which was the first bus registered in the county of Inverness. This was in May 1910 and it was a Halley 24 h.p. model finished in a yellow livery with blue lining. It is seen at Temple Pier, Drumnadrochit, from where the tourist passengers returned to Inverness by boat on Loch Ness. As may be noticed the main road (now the A82) to Fort William at that time had an unmetalled earth surface which could be a dustbowl in dry weather and a quagmire in the wet.

Town services in Inverness had been run by Wm. Greig since the 1920s but in 1947 he sold to Walter Alexander who continued operations until 1952 when they passed to newly formed Highland Omnibuses. The majority of the Greig fleet was an assortment of elderly Leyland TD1s, several originally with Sheffield Corporation like WE 8780 of 1930 seen in Academy Street still in wartime livery with the driver holding a plaque denoting its service in 1941 with London Transport (the furthest travelled bus to help out in the Metropolis). This became R564 with Alexander but did not survive to H.O.L. ownership.

In the 1950s and 60s Inverness town services were operated by a quite remarkable assortment of buses many of which had been cascaded down from other members of the Scottish Bus Group. Crossing the old Ness Bridge in the late '50s we see J153 (WG 3486) which was a 1935 Alexander bodied Leyland TD4 (originally a single decker) inherited with Alexander's Inverness based fleet on the formation of H.O.L. in 1952. Destination reads Laurel Avenue via Ballifeary.

The present Ness Bridge dates from September 1961. Between the closure of the old bridge and opening of the present one, this temporary structure was in place. With a backdrop of Inverness Castle we see J154 (SN 7136) which had started life with David Lawson of Kirkintilloch as a single decker in 1936 before receiving a new double deck body in 1943, passing to Alexander and ultimately to Highland.

In 1962 Highland took over the services of Donald MacKay & Sons of Tain. Their main route ran to the fishing village of Portmahomack at the mouth of the Dornoch Firth, where a Willowbrook bodied Leyland Tiger PS1 passes the Co-operative store (now a restaurant). Highland did not retain MacKay's buses but ORE 641 later worked on the Isle of Lewis for Galson-Stornoway services of Lower Barvas.

One of several acquisitions in 1964 was the old-established business of W.D. MacKenzie, Garve Hotel, Ross-shire. Two buses, one minibus, one van and the hotel were taken over. On arrival in Ullapool from Inverness is a 1955 Albion Victor with Strachan body which became A9 with Highland and operated until 1968. The hotel did not receive a fleet number but remained under Scottish Bus Group control until 1977.

G9 was an Alexander bodied Volvo/Ailsa which had been new to Alexander (Fife) in 1975, passing to Highland in 1980. Based at Thurso depot, it is seen on Scrabster pier connecting with the P. & O. Orkney mailboat *St. Ola*.

Highland Omnibuses Ltd. became Highland Scottish in 1985 (or Highland Scottische as it was more familiarly known by irreverent employees). Posed on the banks of the River Ness with Inverness Castle above is N4 a Leyland National 2, one of eight which arrived in 1980 mainly to work the Inverness town services. This one had an interesting career, later passing to Kelvin then Fife Scottish Omnibuses and is still operating with Stagecoach Red & White in Cwmbran.

Along with 10 other Alexander Y type bodied 1971 Leyland Leopards, L3 came north in 1981 from Western S.M.T. This one ran for only two years with Highland and is seen at Tain post office working the main road route to Inverness.

Aberdeen Corporation

Aberdeen's choice of buses in the 1920s was divided between Thornycroft and Albion. One of the latter, no. 38 (RS 8058) bodied by Northern Counties in 1927 looks diminutive between the two Corporation tramcars outside the Music Hall in Union Street. Tram 112 on the route from Bridge of Dee to Bridge of Don was new in 1925 with body by Brush of Loughborough and lasted until final tramway operation in 1958.

The last Albions purchased by Aberdeen Corporation were eight 'Valkyries' in 1935. Seen when new in Balnagask Road Garden City on service 18 is no.36 whose body was built locally by Walker of Aberdeen, who constructed several batches of both single and double deckers for the Granite City municipality.

A wartime delivery in 1943 was Massey bodied Daimler no.136 with 5 cyl. Gardner engine. Close behind as they head west along Aberdeen's main thoroughfare, Union Street, is 81, a 6 cylinder model of 1947 with Daimler's own engine and body by Northern Coachbuilders of Newcastle-on-Tyne.

No. 26 was a Weymann bodied A.E.C. Regent III RT type of 1947, seen turning from Guild Street to Market Street on service 17 to Torry. It carries the original style of destination layout which was later altered to single line configuration with a separate route number display.

Leaving Kincorth to enter Great Southern Road on service 16 to Garden City is 101, a 1950 Weymann bodied Daimler CVG6. Aberdeen Corporation was the most northerly municipal transport operator in Britain and their fleet was always well maintained and attractive in its smart green and cream livery.

An advert from a visitor's guide book to Aberdeen which featured one of the Corporation's ten Crossley coaches of 1950 bodied by Brockhouse of Clydebank, although appearing more like a Maudslay than a Crossley.

No. 181 (GRG 181) was a 1954 Daimler CVG 6 with Crossley bodywork seen in Union Street on service 23 to Mastrick, with an Austin 'K' type van alongside. 181 later operated for Greyhound of Arbroath. The tram rails are still in position, but the overhead wires have been removed, dating this view to the late 1950s.

Part of a batch of 15 Metro-Cammell bodied A.E.C. Regent Vs delivered in 1958. Visible in this view before entering service at the King Street depot are 255-263 (KRS 255-263)

Dundee Corporation

Dundee Corporation operated a trolleybus service from 1912 which lasted less than 2 years. 67 and 68 were solid tyred Railless trolleys with Milnes, Voss bodies which were used on a route along Clepington Road linking the Downfield and Maryfield tram services. This view at Maryfield shows 68 with destination 'Fairmuir'.

Apart from demonstration vehicles, Dundee's first double deckers arrived in 1931. These were 12 all-Leyland Titan TD1s and some of these may be seen in this view of Shore Terrace Bus Stance, which also shows the now-demolished Royal Arch. Prominent on the right is no. 35 (TS 9117) which was the first of the batch.

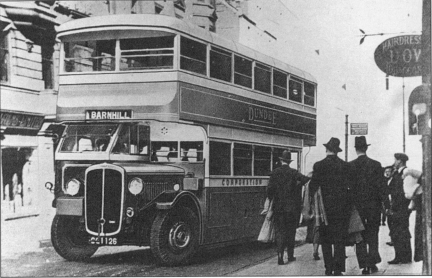

A double deck demonstrator (CG 1126) which arrived in 1932 painted in full Corporation livery was this Thornycroft Daring whose bodywork by the Gloucester Railway Carriage & Wagon Works presented a rather ungainly appearance. Five Darings were purchased later that year, but with Metro-Cammell bodies.

Dundee's fleet generally seemed to present a somewhat 'tired' image in post war years. Municipal standards in the Tayside city were apparently not so high as those of the other Scottish Corporation Transport systems. At the city stance in the early 1950s we see 99 & 100, Daimler COG6 models of 1939 with locally built bodywork by Dickson of Dundee.

The first single deckers since 1938 were delivered in 1947. Numbered 1 & 2, they were A.E.C. Regals with Weymann bodywork and this view at Claverhouse terminus in 1957 shows no.1, with the conductor perched on the bonnet chatting to the driver.

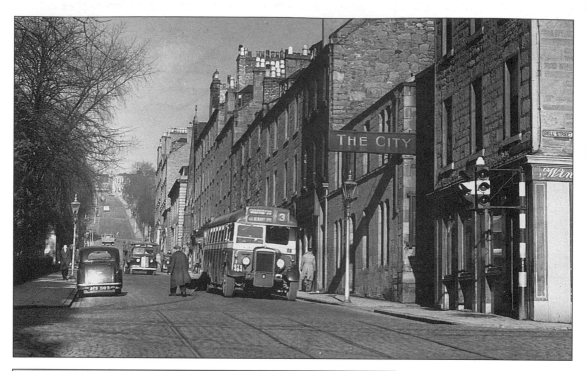

1951 deliveries were all Daimlers, the deckers with bodies by Croft and the singles by Brush, represented here by no.14 on service 3 in Constitution Road approaching the Bell Street junction. Dundee's last trams had run in October 1956 but the Hilltown route tracks are still in place in this late 1950s scene.

To replace the abandoned trams a fleet of former London Transport A.E.C. Regents was purchased in 1955/6. First to arrive were ten Weymann bodied STLs dating from 1946 and seven of these, still in L.T. livery are seen at Dock Street depot prior to entering service. With the arrival of new Alexander bodied Daimlers, all the STLs were withdrawn in 1964.

In 1956 the remainder of the former London buses arrived. These were thirty Craven bodied RT types and gave yeoman service in the Tayside city, all running until the late 1960s. 234 leaving the city for Fintry exemplifies these fine vehicles.

Edinburgh Corporation

Among the first municipal buses in Edinburgh were these two solid-tyred Leylands, nos. 5 & 15 (S 9310/20) which came in 1919. On a summer Sunday the following year we see them on shuttle duties between the Zoo and its nearest tram terminus, which at that time was Murrayfield. Cable car 213 is about to return from there towards the City, while police control the lengthy bus queue.

In 1920 this Y type A.E.C. was one of 30 bodied by Hora of London. No.157 (SG 2008) descends the Mound with its solid tyres fitting neatly into the cable-car rails, while through the mist rises the famous Princes Street skyline, with the Scott Monument to the left and the North British Hotel to the right.

Dunsapie Loch in the Queen's Park provides the background to this view of SF 6029, a trim little 14 seat Dennis charabanc bodied by Vickers of Crayford, one of three ordered for city tour work in 1926.

Leyland Lions were delivered to the Corporation both in 1926 and '27. No. 512 was the first of the 1927 batch and had dual entrance bodywork by Croall of Middlefield, Edinburgh. Location is the foot of the Mound, bound for Blackhall and Davidson's Mains. Edinburgh's rich red livery, officially described as madder, remains the same today.

The black basalt of Edinburgh Castle rock looms behind Cowieson bodied Daimler no.33 as it rounds Johnston Terrace on service 4 shortly after delivery in 1930. The sign on the pole to the right is not a bus stop but reads 'Please do not spit on the pavement'.

Three Morris Dictators with bodies by Mitchell of Cranstonhill, Glasgow, were also added to the fleet in 1930. No.48 takes a rest between runs at Murrayfield Road in the upper class area of Ravelston Dykes on lightly trafficked service 15 to Bernard Street.

In the post-war years, Daimlers were again a popular choice with Scotland's capital transport system. Metro-Cammell bodied A92, delivered in 1948, hurries along Princes Street en route to Juniper Green passing tram 64 heading the other way for Liberton. Currently, Lothian Region Transport is Britain's largest remaining council-owned bus company.

Granton Square on the shore of the Firth of Forth. In years gone by, Granton Harbour was the busy terminal for ferries across the Forth to Burntisland in Fife. 1951 saw Leyland Royal Tiger 801 (JFS 524) join the fleet, seen here on service 17 to Muirhouse. Its otherwise modern lines appear somewhat antiquated by the traditional rear entrance of the Alexander body.

A far cry from today, this was a very peaceful Charlotte Square in 1954 when granite setts paved the streets and 451 was a brand new Leyland Titan. A grand total of 200 of these Metro-Cammell bodied PD2/20s were delivered for tramway replacement services in 1954-5, with a further 100 following later. The remaining city tramway system was finally substituted by buses in November 1956.

Princes Street is arguably the most famous thoroughfare in Britain. A wealth of transport interest fills this scene from summer 1955, with the Castle dominating the skyline. At Jenners corner is Guy Arab 336 bound for Bingham which had started life in wartime with London Transport as their G258, but rebodied for Edinburgh by Nudd Bros. & Lockyer of Kegworth, Leicestershire in 1952. Two of the tram replacement PD2/20s follow, led by 481, while heading west is 248, an all-Leyland PD2/12 of 1952. The trams are 150 on service 6 and 208 on service 9.

Glasgow Corporation

For such a major city, Glasgow was late (1924) to introduce buses to the municipal transport system, mainly because the tramways had coped admirably till then. As Corporation housing schemes spread, so the bus fleet grew and in 1928 nearly 100 Leyland 'deckers arrived. Ten Cowieson bodied Albion single deckers were also purchased, the last of this make for 11 years. 25 & 26 climb steep Gardner Street in Partick on pre-delivery test from the nearby Albion works at Scotstoun.

Successive batches of Leyland Titans were delivered over four years from 1928, the majority with Glasgow built bodywork by Cowieson of St. Rollox. 203 was a 1930 example and when withdrawn from Corporation service in 1944 was sold to Caledonian of Dumfries, ultimately passing to Western S.M.T. where it ran as their 905 until 1955.

In 1935-6, 50 Cowieson bodied Albion Venturers arrived with the first new diesel engines in the fleet (1-20 from Gardner and 21-50 with Beardmore units). No. 5 bustles back to Larkfield Garage on a depot working of service 2, passing the post office in George Square.

A.E.C.Regents found favour again in 1937 and each year thereafter until 1940. One of this last batch was Weymann bodied 745 leaning as it turns from Broomielaw to cross Glasgow Bridge over the Clyde. Also visible in this view from the late 1940s are Standard and Cunarder type trams, one of the former on service 8 to Giffnock passing Ross's dairy in Jamaica Street.

The first deliveries after the utility Guys and Daimlers of wartime were Albion Venturers in 1947. Earlier that year, however, there was also a solitary Crossley, with that company's own bodywork and Brockhouse turbo-charged automatic transmission. This non-standard equipment had been replaced by a conventional gearbox by the time of this mid 1950s view of C1 in Maxwell Street. Withdrawn in 1957, it served for a further 6 years with AA Motor Services member Dodd's of Troon.

Knightswood Garage in 1949 when many of the buses visible were shortly to be withdrawn, including the Pickering bodied Guy Arabs on the left and the Cowieson (466) and Weymann (490) bodied Leyland TD5s on the right. Third from left L18 was originally a Cowieson bodied TD5 of 1935 which had received a new Alexander body in 1949.

Another batch which received new bodies included 1938 A.E.C. Regents. In a cobbled George Square in the early 1950s is AR277, heading for the then infant Drumchapel housing scheme. The original Cowieson bodywork had been replaced by Scottish Aviation at Prestwick Airport in 1950. Most G.C.T. buses registered in 1938 appropriately carried 'BUS' index marks, this one being BUS169.

Glasgow Corporation introduced trolleybuses in 1949. Two of the initial fleet pass on service 102 at the top of High Street, Townhead. TB19 heads for Polmadie while TB21 climbs towards Riddrie. Both were B.U.T. trolleys with Metro-Cammell bodywork. The trolleybus fleet peaked at 194 in 1959 when the system was Britain's 3rd largest.

The last batch of trolleybuses arrived in 1958, both double and single deckers. TB111 was a B.U.T. with Crossley body, on service 105 to Clarkston in St. Vincent Place at George Square. The final trolleys operated in May 1967 and their depot at Hampden then closed.

B38 (EGA 44) was a Metro-Cammell bodied Albion Venturer of 1949 on service 37 from Springburn to Aikenhead pursued down High Street past Provand's Lordship by TD22, one of the Daimler trolleybuses delivered the same year, also with Metro-Cammell bodies and outwardly identical to the 'TB' series. Note the green roof on B38, a short-lived livery feature which existed only in the immediate post war years.

The once-familiar view from the balcony of the old St. Enoch railway station, now home to St. Enoch shopping centre. At the bus stance in the mid 1950s are Daimlers D57 of 1951 bodied by Alexander and wartime DR27 with East Lancs body which had replaced the original by Brush. Also visible are two Lowland Motorways coaches on their service to Renfrew Airport.

In 1950 the last delivery of attractive Metro-Cammell bodied A.E.C. Regents arrived. Among these was A152, seen in Royston Road on service 11 from Robroyston Hospital to Yoker. Glasgow's colourful orange, green and cream livery with black wings which had been in use since the inception of the city buses was more attractive than any of the colour schemes used subsequently.

Until Hillington railway bridge on the main Glasgow/Paisley line was replaced in 1964 double deckers could not pass below to reach Hillington Industrial Estate. Service 25 between the Estate and Govan Cross was therefore maintained by some of a fleet of 43 Daimler single deckers like DS22, whose bodies were built by G.C.T. themselves at Larkfield bus works between 1948 and 1952.

The only other Daimler single decker was very different. This was DS44 of 1953, bodied as a 32 seat 'standee' type by Alexander which originally had an open centre doorway as seen, before later conversion. The 'Freeline' had a relatively short life with G.C.T., being withdrawn in 1962.

Representing the recent bus scene in Glasgow are three Leylands and a Volvo, all bodied by Alexander of Falkirk and seen during severe weather conditions in February 1995 when Great Western Road flooded at Kirklee. Fronting the foursome is Olympian LO 71 with Atlantean LA 1189 behind. On the right is Volvo Citybus AH 10. A special event to commemorate Glasgow's final Atlantean was held in June 1998, marking the end of a span of 40 years.

Perth & Kilmarnock Corporations

The Almondbank Motor Bus.

Perth Corporation operated both trams and buses. Horse trams were replaced by electric cars in 1905 and in 1911 motor buses were introduced initially as feeders to the tram system between the Dunkeld Road terminus and Almondbank and from Craigie to Bridge of Earn. The original buses were Belhavens built in Wishaw, one of which poses at Almondbank post office.

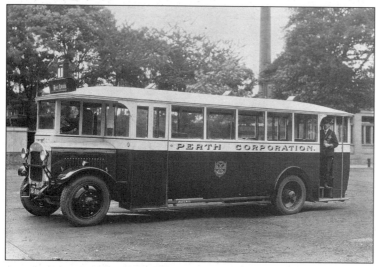

This was one of ten Thornycrofts of mixed type which arrived in 1928. GS 368 had dual entrance bodywork by Ransomes of Ipswich. The final tram ran in 1929 and municipal control ceased in 1934 when an arrangement was made with Walter Alexander to operate the former Corporation services. Alexander's Perth fleet was painted in a red livery as distinct from their normal blue and lettered 'Perth City Transport' (see p. 33). This bus became O249 with Alexander.

Scotland's smallest municipal operator was Kilmarnock Corporation. Trams had started here in 1904 (ending 1926) but the first buses did not appear until 1924 when four of these 20 seat Albions bodied by Stewart of Wishaw entered service between the town centre and Bonnyton. The smart livery was dark green with yellow band and white roof. In 1932 the Killie buses passed to control of the newly established Western S.M.T. Co. Ltd.

Since Scotland is such a scenic country, many operators have taken advantage of the opportunities to provide tourist services, including Sanderson Bros. of Glasgow. At Crianlarich Hotel in June 1924 is HS 3152, an Albion Viking bodied by Simpson of Bridgeton which was a typical charabanc of the period with a door to each row of seats, a fold-down hood and a running board, the appearance of which provides the impression of a large luxury motor car. Prior to purchase by Sanderson, this Viking had been Albion Motors' demonstration model and had appeared at the London Olympia motor show when new in 1923.

A busy scene at the foot of the Mound, which was used as a tours stance in Edinburgh in the early 1920s. To cater for the huge demand for day excursions (few folk had their own transport then), S.M.T.'s own build of 'Lothian' charabancs line up on the right for Carlops, with a Thornycroft in the foreground for the Forth Bridge. On the left, White's Halley (SG 2109) has a full load for a suburban tour for 3/- (15p) while to the rear one of their Clyde charas loads for Peebles for 7/- (35p).

For destinations further afield, extended tours were popular and when this view was taken in 1930, reaching the Isle of Skye involved two ferry crossings as there was no bridge across Loch Long at Dornie. S.M.T. operated an extensive programme of these tours but because of various restrictions on many of the Highland roads, 14 seat vehicles were the maximum permitted. Chevrolet SC 7517 was in this category, with body by Alexander Motors of Edinburgh and is seen on Dornie Ferry with the village visible beyond. This coach ran latterly with Skye operator Sutherland of Broadford until 1947.

Alexander's 'Royal Blue Coaches' as they were known during the 1930s also offered a selection of extended tours which included the Isle of Skye. This mid 1930s view shows the jagged peaks of the Cuillin mountain range from Torrin on the road between Broadford and Elgol, dwarfing diminutive W18 (WG 2350), a 1934 Bedford WLB which carried a specially built 14 seat body which was one of the smallest ever constructed by Alexander at their Drip Road coachworks in Stirling.

Alexander's also ran an extensive programme of day and afternoon tours from Glasgow. As late as the 1960s, mystery tours proved popular with Glaswegians and on busy days even elderly service buses such as Stepps based P659 which was a 1940 Leyland Tiger TS8 would be pressed into tour duties from Alexander's Glasgow office in Cathedral Street.

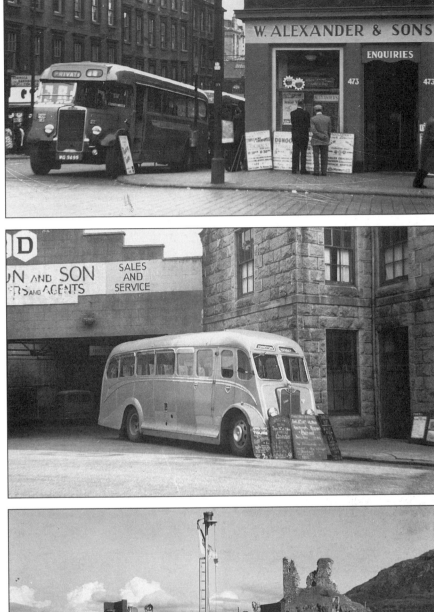

The 1960s saw an end to many of the traditional family-owned small coaching businesses, such as Thos. Johnston & Son of Dalbeattie, Kirkcudbrightshire, who ceased trading later in that decade. In the summer of 1962, Guy Vixen DFR 518 sits outside his garage in the town with boards advertising various excursion destinations, one of which promotes a 3-day Scarborough, Harrogate and Blackpool tour. The 29 seat body on this 1948 coach had been built by Ormac of Walmer Bridge near Preston, one of numerous small firms which supplied a need during the peak post-war boom years for the bus and coach industry.

The opening in 1996 of the Skye Bridge between Kyle of Lochalsh on the mainland and Kyleakin on Skye meant withdrawal of the familiar ferries. One of the firms which had operated extended tours to the island for many years was Lawson's Land Cruises of Kirkintilloch, whose C11, a 1949 Scottish Aviation bodied Commer Commando is seen leaving the ferry *Broadford* at Kyleakin in the mid 1950s.

The jewel in Scotland's crown as regards tourism has always been Edinburgh Castle. This view from around 1950 shows a variety of coaches in use at that period in the lee of the Castle. Leading the line are two 1947 A.E.C. Regals. The first (on an extended tour to John O' Groats) was owned by Trent Motor Traction of Derby and has a Windover body, while an Alexander bodied example with S.M.T. is behind. Next is one of thirty Duple bodied Bedford WTBs delivered to S.M.T. in 1937, followed by a Burlingham rebodied 1933 Leyland Tiger, also with S.M.T. At the end is one of the ubiquitous Bedford OB/Duple coaches and another A.E.C. Regal/Duple.

As the years advanced, former Scottish Bus Group companies showed less interest in tour work, leaving this more specialised side of the industry to others. However, Clydeside Scottish, formed in 1985 and thus one of the newer SBG members, dabbled in both day and extended tour operations for a period. Creeping cautiously through cattle on the road near Feshiebridge while on a Strathspey tour in 1986 is 408, a Plaxton bodied Dennis Dorchester which was one of the initial deliveries to the new company and in Citylink livery to operate express services on their behalf.

Purchased by David Dean's Classique tours of Paisley in 1981 with the intention of providing day excursions from the Glasgow area was 203 YTE, a former Lancaster Leyland PD2 of 1963 with East Lancs. bodywork converted to open top in 1977. Negotiating a tight turn from the Portincaple road towards Whistlefield above Loch Long during a test tour, the Titan performed well but the tour series did not proceed.

Three coach tour brochures depicting vehicles from within each fleet. Lawson's 1952 leaflet shows one of the new PB series Alexander bodied Leyland OPS 2s. Harper's Motor Services of Peebles advert has DS1618, a 1930 Thornycroft while Lowland Motorways extended tours brochure for 1956 features JGD 667, a Leyland Royal Tiger with Burlingham 'Seagull' body (see p. 96).

Gone . . . but not forgotten

These words are true of a succession of bus operators in Scotland who have gone out of business over the past few decades. Northern Roadways of Glasgow, Baxter's of Airdrie, Lowland Motorways of Glasgow and Chieftain of Hamilton are but a few classic examples.

Northern Roadways' pedigree only went back to 1941 but their operations until they ceased trading in the late 1970s were full of interest. Initial business involved wartime works contracts, later developing much school and charter work post-war. This Duple bodied A.E.C. Regal was one of five bought in 1946 and is seen at Prestwick Airport on Northern's express service from Glasgow.

A scene from 1952 at Northern Roadways purpose-built depot in Helen Street, Ibrox (now the police garage) showing a selection of the different types of vehicle then in use, all purchased new. A.E.C. Regal 1V JGD 113 was one of twenty similar Burlingham 'Seagull' bodied A.E.C. and Leyland Royal Tiger coaches for use on express services to London, Birmingham and Bournemouth in opposition to a much aggrieved nationalised Scottish Bus Group. The other three were used on contract and school work: Crossley/Scottish Aviation GGB 362; Bedford OWB/S.M.T. AMS 328 and Daimler CVD6/Barnard of Norwich GGE 880.

James Baxter started business in Coatbridge in 1914, his first regular bus service connecting Gartness with Old Monkland a few years later, developing into a network of routes in the Monklands area. Dennis Darts appear to be everywhere these days and so it is interesting to compare the equivalent product in the mid 1920s, when Baxter's operated this little Dennis. The employment of a conductress seems somewhat superfluous on a 14 seater such as VA 4622.

Baxter's 103 was displayed at the 1954 Earl's Court Commercial Motor Show. Not perhaps what it appears at first glance, it was exhibited as a Crossley Reliance and that maker's badge may be seen; bodywork was also by Crossley. On acquisition by Scottish Omnibuses Ltd., it became B12.

Half of the fleet of 52 vehicles on take-over were double deckers. 67-8 were 1957 A.E.C. Regent Vs with Massey bodywork and this Wigan company built 20 new 'deckers for Baxter's from the mid 1950s until their sell-out to S.O.L. in 1962. A tribute to the high regard in which the company was held is obvious as the new owners not only retained the Baxter name and livery for a period but actually repainted some of their own buses in Baxter's blue.

An earlier purchase by Scottish Omnibuses was Lowland Motorways of Glasgow in 1958. This company, whose coaches later carried the 'Greyhound' logo, started in 1928 operating a cross-border service to Manchester. After the war, local services based at a depot in Shettleston were established around the east end of the city with the acquisition of Harry Black of Springboig.

Two of Lowland's early express service coaches: GG 3915 was a Burlingham bodied A.E.C. Regal of 1931 and GE 6001 a Pickering bodied Leyland Tiger TS2 of 1929, both parked outside Lowland's city office in Buchanan Street.

At the same location in Buchanan Street in the early 1950s is a long line of Lowland coaches preparing for day tours, headed by the pride of the fleet at that time – a 1951 Leyland Royal Tiger with Burlingham 'Seagull' coachwork. No.26 (JGD 667) became H105 in the S.O.L. fleet.

Lowland no.35 was their first double decker, seen here at Queenslie Estate shortly after purchase. It was a former Glasgow Corporation Albion Venturer CX 19 of 1939 with English Electric bodywork. This was bought in 1952 for Lowland's expanding east end services.

Lowland's final two buses, seen in the Shettleston Road depot, were the interesting prototype Leyland rear engined 'deckers, known as Lowloaders and which were really the predecessors of the Atlantean. Both STF 90 with Saunders Roe body and XTC 684 with M.C.W. body were bought in 1957, the latter operating in a red livery as distinct from Lowland's standard two shades of green. Neither 62 nor 63 passed to Scottish Omnibuses.

The 'other' Highland in Scotland was Carmichael's Highland Bus Service, latterly of Glenboig in Lanarkshire. Their main route linked Kilsyth and Coatbridge, serving a succession of mining communities and had been started shortly after John Carmichael V.C. returned from the Great War. Walter Alexander & Sons (Midland) finally acquired the business in 1966, having previously purchased part in 1933.

V 6703 was one of the earliest arrivals immediately after World War 1. This was a solid tyred RAF type Leyland charabanc seen at the Meadows in Glenmavis, where the fleet was originally based. John Carmichael, V.C. is on the left.

Plaxton of Scarborough built the body on VD 323, an Albion PMA28 delivered in 1931 for the service between Annathill and Glasgow which was sold to Alexander in 1933. The main livery was red but note also the Stewart of Appin tartan waistband, a popular embellishment which was applied to some of the fleet.

Passing through Sunnyside, Coatbridge in the early 60s towards the end of its journey from Kilsyth is one of several former Western S.M.T. Burlingham bodied Leyland PSIs with Highland, followed by GVA 324 an Albion CX39 with Carmichael's own bodywork.

Chieftain Bus Service of Burnbank, Hamilton, was started around 1924 by John Laurie who concentrated on routes in the area between Hamilton, East Kilbride and Eaglesham. On service between East Kilbride and Auldhouse is Albion no.7 which was purchased from J.W. & R. Torrance of Hamilton who were its first owners in 1927. Chieftain's green livery was relieved by a tartan waistband which was a popular addition at that time in many Scottish fleets.

Negotiating one of East Kilbride's many roundabouts is a Massey bodied Leyland PD3 new to Chieftain as no.69 in 1959 and which became HL209 when the company sold to Central S.M.T. in 1961.

Paisley buddies' buses

Paisley area independents who were once well-known names in the bus world included Cunningham of Paisley, Paton of Renfrew, Garner of Bridge of Weir, Graham of Hawkhead, Smith of Barrhead and McGill of Barrhead, all of whom have disappeared over the years.

Cunningham's Bus Service of Paisley had shared operations on the Paisley to Renfrew Ferry service with Paton of Renfrew since the 1920s and latterly with Western S.M.T. who went on to acquire both companies in 1979. Former Ribble Leyland PD2s are seen in the mid 1960s at the Ferry terminus, with Paton's Tower Garage on the left.

Cunningham's also operated 'Ivanhoe' coaches and an unusual member of this fleet was AGR 975, a 1950 A.E.C. Regal with observation coach body by Whitson of West Drayton. (Remember the Dinky Toy?) Driver Jimmy Craig later became manager.

Joint operation between Paisley and Renfrew Ferry is illustrated in 1957 shortly after closure of the Glasgow Corporation Tramway service over the same route. One of Cunningham's former London Transport Craven bodied A.E.C. RTs loads for Paisley while an ex Chesterfield Corporation wartime M.C.W. utility bodied Guy Arab with Paton Bros. waits at the Ferry terminus for the next departure. Cars queue to cross the Clyde on the chain ferry which has since been replaced by a passenger only vessel.

Private hire work was also important to Paton's and in the immediate post-war years the coach fleet included these three Leylands originally with Alexander of Falkirk (no.4) and Smith of Wigan (no.6) while no.2 was a new Lion bought in 1936. Bodywork on JP 834 was by Santus of Wigan while the others were built by Alexander in their Drip Road coachworks, Stirling. The route number blind of no.2 displays the message 'Tae a' Airts an Pairts'.

Graham of Hawkhead operated a fleet consisting almost exclusively of Guy Arabs during the 1950s & 60s. No. 56, with Paisley registration FXS 601 approaches Hawkhead terminus in 1962 when new. This example of the 'Johannesburg' style was built by Strachan and was Graham's last purchase of a new Arab. Graham's livery was similar to that which had been used by Young's Bus Service of Paisley. When Y.B.S. sold to Western, Graham adopted the orange colours to replace their former red.

Further second hand deliveries of Guy Arabs arrived during the 1960s including 59 which was one of several from Southampton Corporation. It is seen in Penilee en route from Govan to Linwood. The main services linking Hawkhead, Paisley and Govan Cross to Linwood enjoyed almost mushroom growth when the Rootes Group chose to establish their car plant there but nevertheless Graham's simply relinquished the business in 1990.

McGill of Barrhead moved operations from Ayrshire to Renfrewshire in 1933 and ran from Barrhead to Paisley until selling out to Clydeside Buses in 1997 (although the McGill name has been retained in the meantime by new owners Arriva). CHH 745 was a 1948 Albion CX19 with a second hand Eastern Counties body which had come from Blair & Palmer of Carlisle in the mid 1950s. The crew pose with the Venturer at the Barrhead (Glasgow Road) terminus of the service to Paisley.

McGILL'S

Better remembered, perhaps, were several all-Leyland Titans in the McGill fleet, like EHS 993 of 1951 seen climbing towards Glenfield en route to Auchenback with the Paisley suburb of Potterhill behind. Although the trams had been withdrawn from this route in 1957 the rails were still in position when this view was taken in 1966.

Also based in Barrhead was James Smith who since the 1920s had connected the Nitshill area with Paisley. In 1947 Smith sold to the Scottish Co-operative Wholesale Society who continued to operate using his name and green/cream colours until 1968 when Western S.M.T. took over. In 1961 S.C.W.S. had added a pair of Park Royal bodied A.E.C. Bridgemasters to the fleet of 9 'deckers, (none of which were to be used by Western.) 30 EGD is seen in Lonend, Paisley on the short run to Todholm.

Dunbartonshire

The buses of Garelochhead Coach Services Ltd. served the area between Helensburgh, Garelochhead, Kilcreggan and Coulport, while the Royal Naval bases on the Gareloch and Loch Long provided a large amount of contract work for their coaches. Over the years G.C.S. operated different types of former London buses including A.E.C. RF types, Merlins, RTs and even a 3 axle 'Q'.

DGO 500 dated from 1937 and was the only 3 axle 'Q' type built. Bodywork was by Park Royal and it was originally intended for 'Green Line' coach services but used for London Country bus work instead. It travelled north to Garelochhead in 1947 when the company was owned by Henry Brown. The destination display reads RHU/GULLY FERRY/SHANDON.

Also from London Transport came Craven bodied A.E.C. RT JXC 172, seen leaving Garelochhead for Helensburgh on the company's main service. This was the first of five to arrive in 1956 and more followed in 1958. In 1980 Garelochhead Coach Services gave up business and their familiar green and cream fleet became yet another memory of erstwhile prominent Scottish independents.

Even in the 1920s London style buses had operated on the Gareloch route. These 'S' type open top 'deckers bodied by Ransomes of Ipswich were owned by the Dumbarton General Omnibus Co. who ran from Dumbarton via Helensburgh to Garelochhead. SN 2888/2891 are seen at Rhu, or Row as the spelling was then.

Lanarkshire

Hamilton (Hammy) Jackson of Auchenheath had operated the service between Lanark and Lesmahagow (and formerly to Strathaven) from the mid 1920s until selling out to Whiteford of Lanark in 1962. GSF 337 in its blue and cream colours was one of four former Edinburgh Corporation Roe bodied Crossleys, seen at Auchenheath post office bound for Lanark in the wintry conditions of December 1962.

Wilson's Gala Motor Transport, based in Whitelees, Lanark, operated services from there to Forth, West Calder, Fauldhouse, Biggar and Shotts in the late 1920s with a fleet which included Reos, Commers and Dennises. This pre-delivery view at dealer Oswald Tillotson's Burnley depot shows second hand forward and normal control A.D.C.s along with a Dennis. Gala was acquired by Central S.M.T. in 1932 but later the Wilson family re-started and are still in operation today based at Carnwath.

The red and cream of Stokes' Bus Service is still well known in the Lanark area. Throughout the 1960s Leylands formed the backbone of the fleet and this view at Stokes' base in Carstairs Village shows two of their Titans. ECK 870 was a 1951 PD2 formerly with Scout of Preston while EUF 162 had originally served with Southdown and was a Park Royal bodied TD7 already 23 years old when it came to Stokes in 1961.

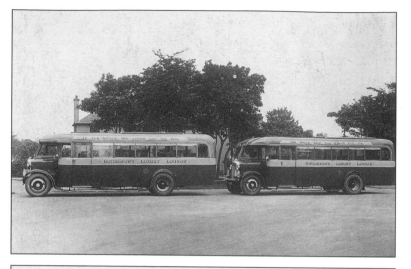

Hutchison of Overtown commenced operations in 1918 and in the mid 1920s became a member of the Lanarkshire A1 Co-operative group on the service between Newmains and Glasgow. In addition to their Motherwell and Wishaw local routes an express service is still operated to Glasgow today. Charter and tour work has also featured strongly in the Hutchison operations and VD 2601-2 were the latest coaches in 1933 when 'Hutchie' as the company was always known bought these two Gilfords with locally built Stewart bodies. Their signwriting reads 'Hutchison's Luxury Lounge' on the waistbands and 'To the Rivers, the Lochs and the Sea' on one side of the roof and 'The Hills and the Glens for me' on the other.

Representative of Hutchison's crew-operated service bus fleet during the 1970s when the company standardised on the A.E.C. Reliance is KVA 561L, a Willowbrook bodied example of 1973. It is seen in the long established blue and cream livery on their service 4 at Flemington heading towards Motherwell from Wishaw in the days when the now closed local steelworks were still in production.

Among the Lanarkshire independent owners who operated double deckers was Adam Duncan of Law who ran the service between Wishaw, Law and Carluke. DVA 670 was a Crossley product of 1947, with Manchester style streamlined bodywork also by Crossley. It later operated until the mid 1960s with Hugh Love of Lesmahagow.

J. & J. Leith of Sanquhar, Dumfriesshire, operated locally to Kirkconnel and also a lengthy journey linking Lanark, Abington, Leadhills and Sanquhar. There was a connection with the S.M.T. service from Dumfries to Edinburgh as seen on a summer Sunday evening in 1962 at Abington where Leith's Leyland Cheetah WG 7620 of 1939 (formerly Alexander's K80) meets B541 of S.M.T., a 1956 A.E.C. Monocoach along with an Austin Metropolitan. Both buses carried Alexander bodywork.

A scene which shows the typical rural nature over most of Leith's route, which passed through Wanlockhead, Scotland's highest village at nearly 1400' above sea level. This 1966 view shows Sanquhar bound Crossley KSM 40 in the Mennock Pass with the Lowther Hills behind. The interesting bodywork was a combination of the original cab and front end by Santus of Wigan and the passenger section from a former Alexander bodied Leyland Cheetah similar to that in the photo above. Leith relinquished this uneconomic service in the 1980s and in 1997 gave up business entirely.

Stagecoach

Another well-known name in the bus industry until finally selling out to Stagecoach in 1985 was A.& C. McLennan of Spittalfield who had developed services in that area of Perthshire after acquiring the businesses of Wm. Armstrong's Spittalfield & District Motor Services (for whom he had been foreman) in 1945 and Allan & Scott of Stanley the following year.

Armstrong's fleet included Fords, Leyland Cubs and Thornycrofts and amongst the Fords was this unusual example from 1929 which had a chassis conversion to forward control by Alexander Motors of Edinburgh who also built the 'sun saloon' bodywork. It operated on the Spittalfield – Perth and Spittalfield – Blairgowrie services which passed to McLennan.

Sandy McLennan made many interesting second hand purchases including eight former London Transport Leyland Titans such as RTL47 in 1958 to which platform doors were added in the Spittalfield workshops (McLennan's also built some complete bodies). In the fleet livery of dark blue and grey it has much more passenger appeal when seen in Perth alongside Alexander's wartime Guy Arab RO699 which co-incidentally was also an ex-London vehicle and had also been built by Park Royal.

In 1980 McLennan's service between Perth and Errol was the first acquisition made by the then fledgling but now giant Stagecoach concern, whose world-wide headquarters are still in Perth. This was their first move into regular service bus operation which has continued to mushroom since then, with continuous upgrading of the huge fleet. FES 831W, a Duple bodied Volvo B 58 of 1980 was the first new bus to be purchased by Stagecoach and is seen in Stanley on the Spittalfield to Perth route in 1988. This vehicle although withdrawn from service has now been preserved by the company.

Stagecoach is also now the owner of what were the two major Ayrshire independent co-operative companies, AA Motor Services and Ayrshire Bus Owners (A1 Service). Originally A1 Service on its own, the company had been formed in 1925 by a joint parnership of many small operators on various routes in Ayrshire. Later some owners left to form AA (Ayr-Ardrossan) and CCS (Clyde Coast Services) who ran Saltcoats to Largs.

Driver Angus Drysdale and Conductress Meg Martin pose proudly beside SL 1602 a Belgian built Minerva of 1931 which was one of the early A1 buses on the Kilmarnock-Ardrossan service. It had been bodied by Cadogan of Perth for original owner Ferguson of Alva and ran briefly between Dollar and Stirling before sale to A1 founder member Drysdale of Dreghorn who later gave up his share in 1934.

EOG 280 was a former Birmingham Corporation Metro-Cammell bodied Leyland Titan TD6C with A1 member Hunter of Kilmarnock and seen in the mid 1950s at the Ardrossan terminus in Parkhouse Road, where the sign on the wall reads 'Kilmarnock bus leaves bay no.1; Shore Road Stevenston bay no.2; Springvale bay no.3'. Behind is CS 8016, a Pickering bodied Albion Valkyrie of 1938.

At the same location a few years later is WCS 196, a Strachan bodied A.E.C. Regent Mk.V bought in 1963 by joint members Kerr & Linney of Ardrossan.

109

CS 8680 was a Pickering bodied Albion Valkyrie coach which operated for AA Motor Services member Dodds of Troon and appeared at the Kelvin Hall Scottish Motor Show when new in 1938. Note the splendid Albion Motors sunrise trademark painted on the radiator grille. This photograph was taken outside their Scotstoun factory prior to delivery.

Operating on the Annbank service when photographed in River Street, Ayr in the early 1950s is a Northern Counties bodied Bristol K5G also owned by Dodds of Troon, whose fleet number DT7 is just visible. This had been an 'unfrozen' wartime delivery to Edinburgh Corporation in 1942 but looks quite at home in the green and cream postwar livery of AA (their pre-war colours had been been red and cream).

The other break-away group from A1 was Clyde Coast Services who operated the Saltcoats-West Kilbride-Largs route. Originally with London Transport, KGK 779 was a Craven bodied A.E.C.RT with member John Hogarth of Ardrossan seen there in 1964 turning from Princes Street to Glasgow Street. CCS sold this service to Stagecoach in 1995 but continue to operate private hires and tours.

Ayrshire

A little known Ayrshire operator but one who ran for about forty years between Girvan and Ballantrae was Gilbert (known as Gib.) Templeton of Ballantrae. DCS 526 was a Plaxton bodied Commer which operated the service from new in 1950 until the business ceased in 1964.

Rowe of Muirkirk is still a familiar name in the Ayrshire bus world, operating a large number of stage and schools services in the county. In 1949 Thos. Rowe purchased CSD 77, an Austin converted to forward control by the bodybuilder Mann Egerton of Norwich, which permitted 31 seats and full fronted coachwork.

A1 services member Andrew Hunter of Springside took delivery of this attractive Foden coach in 1949, with bodywork by Brockhouse of Clydebank. CSD 711 was later sold to the Isle of Arran where it ran for several further years with Lennox of Whiting Bay.

Buses of the Borders

Running out of Dumfries along the west bank of the River Nith was James Carruthers of New Abbey whose father had started the business in 1920. NHL 127 was an uncommon Atkinson Alpha of 1959 with Plaxton body purchased by Carruthers in 1962 from Simpson of Rosehearty and is seen crossing Southwick Bridge on its journey from Rockcliffe to Dumfries.

Weekend visitors to the village of Sandyhills on the Solway shore prepare to board CRN 981 approaching for Dumfries. This Burlingham bodied former Ribble Leyland PS2 replaced the short-lived Atkinson in 1963. Carruthers' distinctive chocolate and yellow buses served the Solway villages for over 60 years before the business was sold to Peacock of Locharbriggs in 1983. Currently the route is operated by McEwan of Dumfries, who interestingly has revived the former Carruthers livery on his 'Dumfries & District Motor Services' buses.

The two tone red fleet of James Gibson, Moffat has been operating since 1919. Faithful to Albions when they were available, these two views show an example of both pre and post war 'Victors'. DSM 601 dated from 1938 and had unusually styled coachwork which was probably an attempt at ultra modernity by Pickering of Wishaw, while KSM 566 of 1950 was also an all Scottish product with body by Scottish Aviation of Prestwick Airport. This is seen in Moffat High Street at the stance for Gibson's long-established service to Dumfries.

James Clark & Sons of Glencaple started with horse-drawn transport in 1902, progressing within a few years to Albion and Halley charabancs. Their main service linked Glencaple, Kelton and Dumfries and this passed to Western S.M.T. when Clark sold out in 1965. Whitesands stance by the River Nith in Dumfries has always been the traditional departure point for all country buses and in the early 1960s we see Clark's green and cream EN 8540, a former Bury Corporation Roe bodied Leyland PD1 along with one of the firm's Austin FX3 taxis.

The South of Scotland Motor Co., based in Dumfries was owned by Richard Percival of Carlisle. Among the mainly Leyland fleet was HH 2425, a 1951 model 'A', seen dropping passengers outside the Cross Keys Hotel in the village of Canonbie, on Percival's route no.10 from Carlisle on the cross-border service to Langholm. This company sold out to Caledonian of Dumfries in 1931.

R.J. Nichol ceased trading in 1966, having operated rural services from the knitwear town of Hawick since 1932. Bedfords had always been the basis of his fleet and YGD 167 is a 1959 example with 41 seat Duple Super Vega coachwork, seen at the isolated Howpasley terminus on Borthwick Water of the service from Hawick which also linked Roberton and Deanburnhaugh, a route which is now served by a 4-seat postbus.

Another now defunct operator in the Scottish Borders was Adam Atkinson of Morebattle who commenced business on return from the armed forces post war. Rural routes to the market town of Kelso via Heiton and via Linton were served through the 1950s by green liveried DNL 690, a Bedford OB/Duple which on this occasion was battling against the elements to reach Morebattle in 1951.

An older example of a borders bus is SH 3021, a neat little 24h.p. Albion of 1928 owned by French of Coldingham on the Berwickshire coast, from where he had started a service in 1908 (originally Laing of Coldingham) to connect with trains at Reston station. James French stands beside his bus, the 14 seat body of which was built by Chisholm the village joiner, which was a relatively common practice in rural areas at that time, although the result seldom appeared so professional as this one, which looks as good as any from a major builder.

OS 111 was a 20h.p. 2 ton Argyll of 1912 on the service operated by Adam Henry of Ardwell between Stranraer and Drummore in the Rhinns of Galloway. The proprietor himself, who had originally operated a horse drawn coach over this route is standing with 'The Reliable'. History does not record whether the Argyll lived up to its name, but previous operators on this same service had little success in this regard, including the Portpatrick & Wigtownshire Railway Co., who tried it with steam buses. From the 1920s until acquired by Western S.M.T. in 1966, Murray of Stranraer operated the route, which is now covered by Stagecoach.

At the station yard in Stranraer is OS 40, one of a pair of Darracq et Serpollet steam buses which ran in 1907-8 over the same route to Drummore as Henry's later Argyll, seen above. This original bus service was operated by the Portpatrick & Wigtownshire Joint Railway in conection with their own trains, but lasted only 18 months. The 30 seat bodywork was built in the Kilmarnock workshops of the Glasgow & South Western Railway Co.

In the Kintyre peninsula of Argyll, Craig of Campbeltown operates the two-tone red fleet better known as West Coast Motors from 'Benmhor', a former whisky distillery in the 'wee toon'. Today they run the trunk service from their home base to Glasgow, from where they also share services to Aberdeen and to Inverness. In earlier years their main route from Campbeltown terminated at Tarbert, where passengers for Glasgow continued with Link Lines' service. Seen outside the village post office in Clachan on the morning run to Campbeltown is SB 5369, a neat little Leyland Cub of 1937 bodied by Pickering of Wishaw. Founded in 1923, West Coast Motors celebrate their 75th anniversary in 1998.

Thirty years later, Bedfords comprised a major portion of the fleet, including some OB models with the familiar Duple Vista bodywork such as SB 7779 seen climbing away from Tarbert harbour on the service down the sparsely populated east coast of the peninsula to the fishing village of Carradale, which operated only on certain days. The Bedford OB was particularly popular with rural operators and was replaced by the SB model in late 1950.

Also based in Campbeltown was A.& P. McConnachie who, like W.C.M.S. served the route to Tarbert via Tayinloan but in addition operated local services in the 'wee toon' and also ran to Machrihanish on the Atlantic coast of Kintyre. Posed at the picturesque terminus is SB 8250 in the grey and blue fleet livery shortly after delivery in 1950. This was a Leyland Royal Tiger with uncommon Duple 'Roadmaster' bodywork which always reminds me of one of my first Dinky model buses!

On the north west side of the Kintyre peninsula lies the area known as Knapdale where Malcolm McLachlan was based at the village of Tayvallich, operating daily to Lochgilphead and Ardrishaig. In the mid 1960s his small red and cream fleet included HGG 359, a former MacBrayne Thornycroft Nippy of 1950 vintage with Croft bodywork, seen on the shores of Loch Sween heading home on the afternoon service. This bus has since been preserved in its original MacBrayne livery.

In northern Argyll, W.L.O. (Billy) Smith of Easdale ran between this former slate quarrying village and the town of Oban. In 1966 on a wet and windy day at Balvicar Cross Roads, KGB 651, his Duple bodied 1952 Albion Victor has arrived from Cuan Ferry and will take the road signposted 'to Easdale'.

The Clyde coast resort of Dunoon in the Cowal peninsula is the largest town in the county of Argyll and today Stagecoach supplies the transport for the area. During the 1950s & 60s most routes were operated by a mixed fleet of second hand double deckers in the red and cream colours of Graham's Dunoon Motor Services. At the pierhead terminus in 1962 we see XS 4771-2, originally Young of Paisley and subsequently Western S.M.T. Albion Venturers of 1938 vintage (but rebodied by E.C.W. in 1953) and EN 7702, an ex-Bury Corporation (Massey rebodied 1951) Leyland of 1938.

The Ayrshire Bus Owners' Association (A1 Service) opened their own bus station in John Dickie Street, Kilmarnock for their frequent departures serving Crosshouse, Dreghorn, Irvine, Saltcoats and Ardrossan where they had another, albeit smaller bus station at the Parkhouse Road terminus. This was the official opening in Kilmarnock in 1958 with a Northern Counties bodied Daimler CVG6 of Hunter, Dreghorn, in attendance.

Kilmarnock was fortunate in having two bus stations, (whereas Paisley, Scotland's largest town, has never had any.) The Scottish Transport Company built this one in Portland Street in 1924 which continued in use by Western S.M.T. until the present bus station opened in 1974 (also serving A1 operations). This scene from 1936 shows a former Scottish Transport Leyland TD1 departing for Darvel.

As did Kilmarnock, the coastal town of Ayr formerly boasted two bus stations. AA Motor Services used these purpose built premises in Boswell Park, which also served as their head office, while the Western S.M.T. bus station was only a short distance away in nearby Sandgate. In the late 1930s Albions dominated the AA fleet but a Leyland Tiger is also visible in this view.

A bird's eye view of Western's Ayr bus station as it was in the late 1950s showing some of the wide variety of buses then in service, with Albion single and double deckers, Guy Arabs and Leyland PD3s. Today the bus station has altered in layout but remains on the same site with Stagecoach operating both the former Western and AA services from here.

Until Shetland's 'Viking' bus station in Lerwick was officially opened in 1991, Scotland's northernmost purpose-built bus station was in Kirkwall, capital of the Orkney Islands. Buses of four operators may be seen in this mid 1960s view, showing Bedford/Duple with Peace, St. Margaret's Hope; Leyland Tiger PS1/Burlingham of Wylie, Birsay; Bedford SB/Duple of Harvey, Evie and Commer/Scottish Aviation of Laughton, Deerness.

Our capital city did not have a proper bus station until 1957 when the St. Andrew Square location opened, still in use today. Prior to this, buses had parked all around the square at kerbside stances (see pp. 44-6). On the opening week, S.M.T. HH555 a recently delivered Leyland PD2/Park Royal waits at stance 12 prior to departure for Glasgow via Bathgate, a service which then had a 20-minute frequency but today no longer operates.

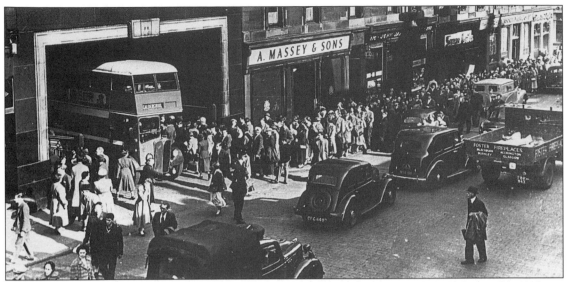

The other end of the previously mentioned service was Glasgow's Buchanan Street bus station, which opened in 1934. This mid 1950s view shows S.M.T. BB45, an Alexander bodied A.E.C. Regent III of 1948 leaving for Caldercruix. Queues such as this which were common then, would warm any traffic manager's heart today.

This glimpse inside Buchanan Street bus station in the late 1950s shows another healthy queue boarding Alexander's Leyland Tiger Cub PD110 bound for Dundee. The present Buchanan Bus Station (street has been dropped) was opened in 1976 and is now the city's only such facility, those formerly at Waterloo Street, Dundas Street and Anderston having closed.

MacBraynes Fort William bus station around 1950. Two post war A.E.C. Regals and a Maudslay, all with Park Royal bodies along with a wartime Bedford OWB/Duple may be seen. The art deco style 1930s building was adjacent both to the town pier on Loch Linnhe and to the railway station. Nowadays the town-centre by-pass along the shore covers this site and the town no longer has a proper bus station.

Stirling has recently benefited by the upgrading of its bus station, seen here in 1944. P408 (WG 5926), an Alexander's Leyland Tiger TS7 of 1937 with wartime masked headlamps and white edged mudguards loads for Glasgow, while an excited small boy dances on one leg (perhaps he's spotted a new utility Guy Arab!)

Falkirk was another town which had two bus stations, but not simultaneously. Alexander's was opened in 1935 at Callander Riggs and remains on this site today, but an earlier bus station was built in 1928 in Cow Wynd by Wilson Marshall's 'Venture' bus company which operated a mainly Thornycroft fleet based in Avonbridge. Most of their routes radiated to areas south of the town from this independent Falkirk bus station, or 'motor service station' as we see on the roof. Alexander took over in 1930 and later closed these premises, retaining the buses and the services.

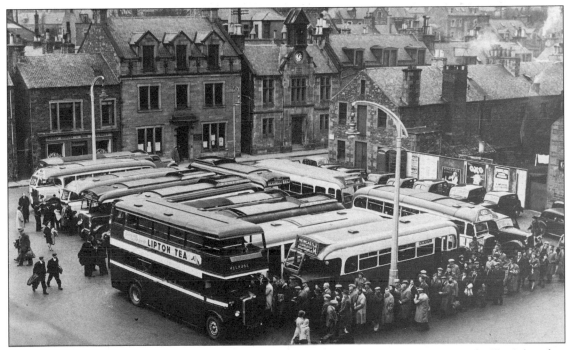

As in many other country towns, buses in Galashiels departed from the town Market Square, which had sufficed since the 1920s despite increasing congestion until the present bus station in Elder Street opened in 1973. This early 1950s scene shows tightly packed lines of mainly S.M.T. A.E.C. Regals and Leyland Tigers, but we can also see a Bristol and a Leyland of United during their lunch stop on service 14 from Glasgow to Newcastle. The double decker is S.M.T. BB20, originally a single deck A.E.C. Regal of 1934 whose Burlingham body was replaced by Alexander in 1944 as seen. Presumably it had been drafted to Gala for the day (it carries the 'A' code for New St. depot) since judging by the queue there was something special happening in Melrose.

The Tale of a 'Q'

The A.E.C. 'Q' type was introduced in 1932 and despite being of a design well ahead of its time (even today it wouldn't look out of place) the orders it deserved were never received. WS 1508 with Weymann body was delivered to Edinburgh Corporation Transport in 1934, when this view at Barnton was taken soon after entering service, gleaming in its municipal maroon (officially described as madder). It was the only one of its type to operate in the capital and stayed until 1945 when it was sold to David MacBrayne, becoming no.53 and based at their depot in Fort William where we see it working on the Corpach service in their colourful red green and cream colours. After five years it passed to Garner, Bridge of Weir and the final illustration shows it towards the end of its life in the early 1950s on the forecourt of their Central Garage which was the terminus of the rural service to Paisley via Georgetown. Garner's livery was a deep red and cream and the 'Q' ran thus for two years before its final run to the scrapman in 1953, having completed an interesting career around Scotland.

Acknowledgements

Much of the information included in the captions has been amassed over the years from owners and employees of just about every bus company in Scotland. Most of the photography is either my own or from my collection but among others deserving credit are: A. W. Brotchie, J. Cairns, K. Cameron, Miss J. Fletcher, J. C. Gillham, G. Jamieson, K. MacKay, I. Maclean, R. Marshall, J. Richardson, W. A. C. Smith, H. Soutter, W. G. Steele, J. Thomson, Quadrant Picture Library. Apologies to anyone unwittingly missed.

The period sketches at both the introduction and on this page have been reproduced from a Link Lines Ltd brochure of 1927, illustrated by the artist W. M. Maxwell. This Glasgow company (controlled by India Tyres of Inchinnan) pioneered the Loch Fyneside service from the city to Ardrishaig and Tarbert that year, operating a fleet of Reo Speed Wagons initially and later progressing to Leyland Tigers.

David MacBrayne entered in opposition over the same route from 1929 and eventually purchased Link Lines in 1932 which was the first of many successive take-overs to build up their West Highland service network.

Both sketches depict one of the original Reos, the introductory one leaving behind grimy Glasgow of the 1920s for the clean air of Argyll.

The photograph taken at the summit of the 'Rest and be Thankful' hill road shows sunshine and shadow in Glen Croe as Reo Speed Wagon GD 6451 pauses before its winding descent. The route board along the side of the roof baggage rails reads 'Glasgow, Arrochar, Inveraray, Lochgilphead, Tarbert'.

ATLANTIC
OCEAN

Shetland

Unst

Ulsta

Lerwick

Sumburgh

THE
NORTHERN
ISLES

Orkney

Kirkwall

Stromness

WESTERN
ISLES

Ness

Stornoway

Lewis

Harris   Tarbert

North
Uist

South
Uist

Portree

Skye

Rum

Tiree

Tobermory

Mull

Islay

Port Askaig

Bute

Rothesay

Arran

Lamlash

Campbeltown

Ardnamurchan

Oban

Inveraray

Greenock

Durness   Thurso   John O' Groats
                 Castletown
                 Watten
                                 Wick

Lairg

Ullapool   Portmahomack

HIGHLAND   Rosehearty

Achnasheen Strathpeffer
Torridon   Peterhead
        Beauly
             Inverness   Huntly
Plockton
        Drumnadrochit   Aberdeen
                    Tomintoul

             Slochd
             Summit
                      Glenshee   Laurencekirk

Fort William   Pitlochry   Forfar
     Kinlochleven
                          Dundee

Crianlarich   Perth   St Andrews

                              Leven
        Stirling
              Dunfermline
        Alexandria Falkirk
              Glasgow Ratho Edinburgh   Coldingham
        Paisley
                  Bonkle   Berwick-
                                      upon-Tweed
        Kilmarnock
                Abington   Morebattle
        Tairlaw   Hawick
        Sanquhar   Moffat

                    BORDERS
                    Canonbie   Newcastle
        Dumfries   Carlisle

Stranraer
             Sandyhills   ENGLAND

Drummore